Open to God: Open to the World

OPEN TO GOD
OPEN TO THE WORLD

POPE FRANCIS

with
ANTONIO SPADARO

Translated by
SHAUN WHITESIDE

BLOOMSBURY CONTINUUM
LONDON · NEW YORK · OXFORD · NEW DELHI · SYDNEY

BLOOMSBURY CONTINUUM
Bloomsbury Publishing Plc
50 Bedford Square, London, WC1B 3DP, UK

BLOOMSBURY, BLOOMSBURY CONTINUUM and the Diana logo are
trademarks of Bloomsbury Publishing Plc

First published in Italy in 2017 as *Adesso fate le vostre domande* by
Rizzoli, Milan © 2017 Rizzoli Libri, S.p.A / Rizzoli, Milano
Preface © Libreria Editrice Vaticana, Città del Vaticano
First published in Great Britain 2018

A catalogue record for this book is available from the British Library

Library of Congress Cataloguing-in-Publication data has been applied for

ISBN: TPB: 978-1-4729-5901-0; ePDF: 978-1-4729-5903-4;
ePUB: 978-1-4729-5904-1

2 4 6 8 10 9 7 5 3 1

Typeset by Newgen KnowledgeWorks Pvt. Ltd., Chennai, India
Printed and bound in Great Britain by CPI Group (UK) Ltd, Croydon CR0 4YY

To find out more about our authors and books visit www.bloomsbury.com
and sign up for our newsletters

CONTENTS

PREFACE

Pope Francis

I'm bold, but I'm also shy. In Buenos Aires I was rather afraid of journalists. I thought they could put me in an awkward position, so I didn't give interviews. But one day I allowed myself to be persuaded by Francesca Ambrogetti, thinking of the good that might come of it. She convinced me, and I trusted her. So once a month, at nine o'clock in the morning, I saw her and Sergio Rubín, and that led in the end to the publication of the interview book called *El Jesuita*. I've always feared negative interpretations of what I say. I didn't like the cover of that first interview as archbishop of Buenos Aires, but I was very happy with everything else. That's how the story of my interviews as archbishop began. I went on to give others to Marcelo Figueroa and Abraham Skorka. Always trusting the people with whom I was speaking.

I was already Pope when Fr Antonio Spadaro came to ask me for an interview. My instinctive reaction was one of uncertainty, as in the past, and I said no. Then I felt that I could trust him, that I had to trust him. And I accepted. I did two long interviews with him, which are collected in this volume. Spadaro is the editor of *Civiltà Cattolica*, a journal that has always been closely linked to the popes. He was present for the interviews and conversations in this book, and transcribed my words.

After that first interview in August 2013 came the others, including the ones that I gave on the plane on the way back from apostolic journeys. Again, on those trips, I like to look people in the eye and answer their questions sincerely. I know I have to be prudent, and I hope I am. I always pray to the Holy Spirit before starting to listen to the questions and giving my answers. And just as I mustn't lose my prudence, I mustn't lose my trust either. I know that this can make me vulnerable, but it's a risk I'm willing to take.

For me, interviews always have a pastoral value. Everything I do has a pastoral value in one way or another. If I didn't have that trust, I wouldn't grant interviews: it's very clear to me. It's a way of communicating my ministry. And I unite those conversations with the daily form of the homilies at the chapel of Santa Marta, which is – so to speak – my 'parish'. I need that communication with people. There, four days a week, 25 people from a Roman parish come to see me, along with others. I have a genuine need for that direct communication with people. Granting an interview isn't like climbing into the pulpit: it means meeting journalists who often ask you questions from the people. Another thing I enjoy is talking to little magazines and popular newspapers. I feel even more at ease. In fact, in those cases I really listen to the questions and concerns of ordinary people. I try to answer spontaneously, in a conversation that I intend to be easily comprehensible, and not using rigid formulas. I also use simple, colloquial language. For me, interviews are a dialogue, not a lesson.

That's why I don't prepare. Sometimes I receive the questions in advance, but I hardly ever read them or think about them. Quite simply, nothing comes to mind. Other times, on the plane, I imagine the questions they might ask me. But to answer, I need to meet the people and look them in the eyes. Yes, I'm afraid of being misinterpreted. But, I repeat, I want to take that pastoral risk. It happens to me in other cases too. Sometimes I've found in my interviewers – even in those who say they are very far away from faith – great erudition and intelligence. And also, in some cases, the ability to be touched by Pascal. That moves me, and I greatly appreciate it.

This book also contains two conversations with the Superiors General of the religious orders. I have always asked them for genuine dialogue. I've never wanted to give speeches, or to have to listen to them. Conversation has always seemed to me to be the real way to meet one another.

In this book there are also a number of conversations with Jesuits. I'm glad that they've been included in this collection. I must say that I feel those moments are very free, especially when they happen during trips: this is my opportunity to reflect on the trip in question for the first time. I feel as if I'm surrounded by my family, and I speak our family language, and I'm not afraid of misunderstandings. So what I say can sometimes be a little risky. I asked Fr Antonio to revise the texts before publication, but I haven't cut anything. In fact, sometimes I feel I have to say what I say to myself, and that's important for me too. In conversations some important things arise that I then think about later. For example, in my meeting with Polish Jesuits I spoke about discernment. On that occasion I became powerfully aware of the specific mission of the Society of Jesus today, which is also a very important mission of the Church for our times.

I want a Church that is able to find its way into conversations between people, a Church that knows how to engage in dialogue. It is the Church of Emmaus, in which the Lord 'interviews' the disciples who have become discouraged. For me, the interview is part of that conversation between the Church and the people of today.

INTRODUCTION

Antonio Spadaro SJ

A WORD THAT KEEPS THE MESSAGE ALIVE

'Let us remember that you need never answer
questions that no one asks.' (Pope Francis,
Evangelii gaudium, no. 155)

It was 13 June 2013. I was waiting, with the other
members of the Community of *Cività Cattolica,* to
be admitted into an audience with Pope Francis in the
Apostolic Palace. It was an audience that every pope
has wanted at the start of his ministry, given the close
traditional link between the journal and the pontiffs.
I was summoned by a *monsignore,* who told me that
the Holy Father was waiting for me, to have a brief
conversation before the audience. I went. It was on
that occasion that I asked Francis for an interview.
He answered with a clear and definite 'No'. And, as
if by way of self-justification, he told me how difficult he found giving interviews. He told me he preferred to think, rather than give on-the-spot answers
in interviews.

Then I saw that he was starting to change his mind.
I saw him in a state of discernment, as if realizing that

it might be a path to travel. So he agreed to answer in writing a series of questions posed in advance, also in writing. In fact, I had the opportunity to hand him my questions (20 of them!) by hand in Brazil, during his visit for World Youth Day, one morning after Mass. But after reading them, once we were back in Rome, he called me to say he preferred to conduct the interview verbally, in a one-to-one dialogue. We agreed the date: 19 August 2013. Then we spent three afternoons going through that interview together.

EYE TO EYE

And Francis really does look you in the eye. 'What I try to do, even today, is look people in the eye', he told me in the interview I had with him in 2016 for a book of all his writings as archbishop of Buenos Aires (*My Word is In Your Eyes*). And he confirms it in the preface that he wrote for that volume. His word is in the eyes of the person or people that he has in front of him. That is, it emerges from a dialogue, it is not prefabricated. We know that there is a freshness to Bergoglio's words thanks to the 'oral doctrine' that he has been giving from Casa Santa Marta since the start of his pontificate.

Reading the present volume, we can see once more that his words are 'broken' in order to be shared at the moment of their offering. There is a vital tension that cannot really be 'domesticated' by being given a finish polish in the workshop. And the context of the interview or the conversation is ideal.

Pope Francis's message is able to touch people immediately, directly, intuitively. His ability to communicate is rooted in pastoral experience, carried naturally to the creation of authentic relationships. His authority is never expressed in a rigid manner, like that of a marble statue; even its physicality is directed towards the interlocutor. And this is apparent even when speaking to him one-to-one in an interview.

The interviewer's words are an inherent part of the interview. They really are, in an authentic relationship with pastoral features. This is clearly apparent, for example, during the press conferences on the aeroplane on the way back from his travels. The Pope's relationship with journalists has the characteristics of a pastoral relationship. Francis confirms this in the piece with which he opens this collection. Obviously every journalist is getting on with their job, and the Pope knows that. But that doesn't stop him – quite the reverse! – from being a pastor. Francis is always 'inside' the communicative event: he creates it and develops it from inside, but without playing out a written role. And that is one of the reasons why he doesn't want to know in advance the questions we are going to ask him. And not only that: several times we have witnessed a kind of 'shilly-shallying', which is why time is sometimes tight for the interviews, because they are conducted on short-haul journeys and the Pope tends to extend them in spite of the limits sometimes imposed by his close collaborators.

Certainly, the fact that Francis doesn't want to know the questions in advance puts the Pope at risk of rambling, because he doesn't have a vague and confected answer prepared in advance. Still, he has the advantage of producing a language that seeks not just to clarify and explain, but also to meet the listener. In this sense he is entirely pastoral. If the language is mimetic, it is because it is brought down to earth, becoming the language of life and not of speculation. The meaning is clear: the evangelical message is to be presented not only as doctrine but also as experience. This is the radical feature of pastoralism. The Pope, as pastor of the Church, feels that it is time for the language of preaching really to be a 'lowered' language, one capable of assuming the same position as the words of Christ, which were spoken not on a glorious throne but by the Son, emptying himself. This is the ultimate motivation for what we see in Francis's interviews and conversations.

Highly significant, in my opinion, is the conclusion of an answer given on the flight back to Rome from the apostolic journey to the Holy Land on 26 May 2014: 'I don't know whether to some extent I have addressed your concerns.' That is Pope Francis's intention when he answers questions: not to deliver definitions and judgements, but to address the concerns of his partner in conversation. And that too is pastoral.

PRIVATE WORDS SPOKEN IN PUBLIC

This volume includes conversations conducted not only one-to-one but also with groups, whether medium-size or very large, of up to 250 people. In these last cases, the Pope is engaging with an assembly. And yet he always answers individual people. It is not an assembly that asks the question, but a single individual. In this case it is immediately apparent how Francis tunes in to the group and seeks the right wavelength. It is visible in his way of standing, his greeting, his physical posture. In the case of the conversations brought together in this volume, the dialogue is with homogeneous groups: the superiors of the religious orders, the Jesuits coming together in the General Congregation. The Pope doesn't appear in front of them as a 'personality', as a star, but he does demonstrate a certain calm, as happened in the second meeting with the Superiors General. All of this helps to 'relax' the assembly after a certain initial excitement. And it helps to focus the dialogue on the real relationship. It avoids the risk of the event being a 'spectacle'. So the answers always relate to the person asking the question, always bearing in mind the context and the group.

One issue in particular concerns the Pope's discussions with the Jesuits during his apostolic journeys. Since his first trip to Brazil, Francis has decided, where possible, to meet the Jesuits of the country he is visiting. This can assume various different forms: a Mass, a personal greeting to a group, a dialogue ... This volume brings together conversations with Jesuits in the Philippines and in Poland, which are significant in terms of both range and themes. Obviously these are private words, not officially recorded and not intended for publication. So these words have been recorded using devices that are not professional, transcribed and then approved by the Pontiff for publication.

In this case the Pope is speaking to his fellow Jesuits. The form of the discussion is highly relaxed, fraternal and spontaneous. And from personal experience I see that these conversations are always an echo of the visit in question. The Pope himself speaks of the experience of these conversations in his preface to this volume. Sometimes they also contain keys to an understanding of the journey itself in the light of the Pope's personal experience. In fact, each apostolic journey has its schedule, which does not allow for shared reflection. These meetings with Jesuits are sometimes an opportunity for the Pope to express what he perceives in the course of the journey, his immediate feelings and considerations.

In this case his word has a very particular force, which gives us a better understanding of something that can also be deduced from other aspects of his pontificate: *Pope Francis needs to be understood on the hoof.* We have to consider the journey that he is accomplishing while he accomplishes it. And the great thing about the interviews and conversations is that they are works in progress. They don't have the necessary rigidity typical of a written text. In this sense the interview and the conversation are a form of expression particularly in harmony with the dynamic forms of this pontificate. In the interview there is always a 'background noise' of life, in one way or another. And this makes a profound difference in the communication of a Pope. Doubt is dispelled not by icy clarity, but by the powerful comprehensibility of the message. Francis asserts this forcefully in his preface to this volume. 'It is the Church of Emmaus, in which the Lord "interviews" the disciples who have become discouraged. For me, the interview is part of that conversation between the Church and the people of today.'

A PERSPECTIVE ON THE PONTIFICATE

What this volume offers to the reader is a particular perspective on the pontificate. What links the interviews is the fact that the person writing was either speaking to the Pontiff or a witness to the conversations. For me it was a precious experience because of the direct contact and the three-dimensionality of the experience, which I attempted to convey in relating the experience itself. I think an interview with Pope Francis needs to be transcribed along with the story of how it actually happened, because it is an event that comes about thanks to an encounter. It isn't enough to record it: it needs to be recounted – sometimes, as with my two long interviews from 2013 (*My Door Is Always Open*, published by Bloomsbury in 2014) and 2016 (*A Shepherd's Footsteps*), inserting the answers into the narration of the context; sometimes, as with the conversations to which I was a witness, illustrating the context in which they took place. This book also includes an interview with the Swedish Jesuit Ulf Jonsson, at which I had the joy of being both witness and interpreter.

What can we deduce from the Pontiff's statements? The only way to answer that question is to read the text. Sometimes what the Pontiff means is better understood with the passing of time, as in the case of my first interview, in 2013. At the time I myself didn't grasp the meaning of some of his statements. Rereading that interview now helps me to gain a deeper understanding of some of Francis's choices, to grasp the extent to which they were part of his vision from the beginning. To give just one example: the importance given to the Synod.

It is still possible to stress some of the aspects of his open discourse that strike me as particularly relevant. Basically, these interviews can be read as if they were a single long conversation over several stages.

Periphery. Francis clearly invites us to look at reality from 'the periphery', because it is from there that changes in history begin. Hence we can easily understand that 'periphery' is not an over-used (and even abused) slogan in the present day. In fact, it is a prophetic category. Peripheries are significant because (and if) they are prophetic, and say something whose meaning 'the centre' cannot provide. 'Be radical in prophecy', the Pope tells the Superiors General in 2016. And he goes on: 'Being radical in prophecy is the famous *sine glossa*, the rule *sine glossa*, the Gospel *sine glossa*. Which is to say: without tranquillizers! The Gospel should be taken without tranquillizers.' The Gospel is not Valium, which puts the conscience to sleep and makes it conform to a given norm; it is a message that shakes and unsettles, that creates movement in the soul, that forces us to go outside ourselves.

Prophecy. The movement of 'going out' is therefore made clearly explicit from the beginning of the pontificate: it is a going out to where human and spiritual meanings can be found. And Pope Francis places a great deal of trust in young people, who are the ones who ask the most demanding questions: 'If young people don't prophesy, the Church lacks air', he says. But they will be able to do this only on one condition that we might call unusual: that old people have 'visions' and dreams. The old person faced with new life, the Pope says, begins to dream. The dream is the distillate of his wisdom. So the young person, if he listens to this wisdom, can face the future and discern meaning. As is quite plain, passing on wisdom has nothing to do with traditionalism or conservatism. Far from it. Past and present interpenetrate to 'see' the future. At the centre is prophecy.

The opposite movement is exemplified by what Francis calls 'clericalism', meaning the hypocritical and superficial adherence to rules, like a deadly and stagnant rigidification. The dialogue with the Philippine Jesuits has the rhythm of going out and the rhythm of the periphery, along with an appeal to take risks, not to become frightened by the challenges that need to be embraced. In the long interview he had with them in 2016 we can see the distant roots of that attitude of Bergoglio's, almost the remote origins of the pontificate in his actions as a parish priest in Argentina, and then as a bishop. In that interview Francis actually says a great deal about himself, about his lived experience. That's why I consider that his answers are fundamental if we are to grasp the origin of his pastoral approach and his way of governing the Church. Reading what Francis says on that occasion, we can discern from a distance the features of the present day. And his statements are important because today Francis is rereading the earlier experiences of Jorge Mario.

Discernment. But we also find the deeper spiritual roots, particularly the importance of discernment. Talking to the Polish Jesuits, for example, the Pope says that 'the Jesuit should be a man with a nose for the supernatural, he should have a sense of the divine and the diabolical with reference to the events of human life and history. The Jesuit must therefore be able to discern both the side of God and the side of the devil.' And he concludes: 'We really need to understand this: in life not everything is black on white or white on black. No! In life shades of grey predominate. So we need to teach people to discern within that grey.' Francis is revealing his vision of life, the picture of a life made of shades, with God acting inside them. A pastor who does not pay attention to shades is not a pastor but an ideologue. But at the same time Bergoglio's lesson in life is also one that gives value not to clear contrasts but to progressions, not to firm and static structures but to developments. These are the vital 'processes'. Speaking to his fellow Jesuits, the Pope acknowledged that this lay at the heart of their charism, and hence also of his own.

Strategy. On the other hand, we still unfortunately encounter attempts to describe Francis's pontificate as disregarding discernment. These attempts like to depict Bergoglio's journey as the obstacle course of one man on his own. The limit of these readings – which give the impression of being useful but which are in fact only naïve or expedient – is that they try to take snapshots of isolated actions of passing moments. The pontificate needs to be read within its development, within the process that it generates, in flux. Anyone who reasons with strategies and objectives according to the most obvious criteria is destined not to understand. So there are those who like to depict Francis as surrounded by a Vatican that has not yet achieved stability, which is often opaque or frantic, lost in the twists and turns of the convoluted old logics.

But Bergoglio's 'strategy' does not respond to those ways of understanding him, which consider him substantially as a man in command, with the goal of stabilization and homogenization. In fact, Bergoglio is a man who is extremely attentive to circumstances and to the dynamism of renewal which is *already* present in them. Francis governs as if he were looking at a complex landscape, seeing simultaneously the elements of stability, the 'mountains', and those of fluidity, the 'waters'. His landscape is complex, and takes many factors into account. Through these conversations it will be easy to grasp this panoramic vision.

Bergoglio waits and considers a situation as it evolves naturally, with all its contradictions, its tensions, including errors and betrayals. Reality moves slowly, and the Pope tries to guide it in the best possible direction, in a way that is unforced and spontaneous. Bergoglio discerns the situation in which he is actually involved, not one reconfigured ideally in his mind. And that is because Francis is a man of faith, and he is convinced that it is God who guides history, giving it impulse and movement.

In his discernment he is able to liberate – and sometimes unleash – the favourable factors, gaining positions on this naturally inclining slope. He also gains them in 'chaotic' situations, which should best be defined as very 'complex'. His government is not expressed in an abstract relationship between theory and practice, but one of the concrete discernment of situations, because he knows that God is at work.

Polyhedron. Another recurring image is that of the polyhedron, the geometric figure that the Pope opposes to the sphere. And this is also the image that holds together not only his vision of a human life but also the events of the world and Francis's understanding of international politics, and indeed the life of the Christian churches. The interview before the apostolic journey to Switzerland is very clear in this respect, and reveals how rich and complex Francis's vision of Christian experience truly is. His ecumenism is not born on the blackboard, but emerges from his keen and friendly relationship with many pastors and theologians of various Christian denominations. What he says in this interview is surprising in many respects. And he helps us to understand that the polyhedron is a figure that expresses very clearly Francis's ecumenism. And – on the basis of his own experience – he says that there is always much to learn. An *ecclesia semper reformanda* is always a learning church rather than a teaching one. We can also learn from crises, from schisms, from conflicts. The important thing is always to look ahead, and not always to be licking the wounds of the past.

Consolation. This collection lacks a dialogue that we want to introduce here because of its brevity. It comes from a meeting with the Korean Jesuits at Sogang University in Seoul, in August 2014. He said to the Jesuits of the Korean province that there is a word by which he is greatly struck: 'consolation'. And that is the movement of the soul which comes from God and guides the Church. It is 'the presence of God in all its modalities. Our Holy Father St Ignatius always tries to confirm the decision of the reform of life or the choice of way of life through the second mode of "choice", consolation. Consolation is a beautiful word for those who receive it. But it is difficult to give consolation. When I read the *Book of Consolation* of the prophet Isaiah,' Francis went on, 'I read that God's work lies in consoling, consoling his people. When someone lives in extreme pain, he knows what to do with love, he becomes a seed of consolation for that person. God's people need consolation, to be consoled, *consuelo*.' Then the fundamental task of the ministry of the Gospel, of the whole Church, is to proclaim to people the mercy and consolation of God. 'I think,' Francis said, 'that the Church is a field hospital at the moment. The people of God ask us to console them. So many wounds, so many wounds need consolation ... We must listen to the word of Isaiah: "Console, console my people!" There are no wounds that cannot be consoled by the love of God. This is how we must live: seeking Jesus Christ, in such a way as to bring that love to console wounds, to heal wounds.' Consolation is the true password that helps us decipher the mystery of the Church.

If, as an interviewer and a witness, I had to say what my personal experience was of these conversations, I would find it very difficult to sum it up. And yet in every circumstance I have perceived on the one hand a sense of great naturalness and normality, and on the other a sense of being in the presence of an erupting volcano. These are two opposing feelings, but which cannot be separated. I trust that the perception of this kind of energetic and generative 'calm chaos' may in some way touch the reader as well.

1

Wake Up the World!
A Colloquium with the Superiors General

When Pope Francis speaks 'off the cuff' and engages in dialogue, his speech has a rhythm like a series of 'waves', which need to be followed carefully because they feed on the active relationship with his interlocutors. Anyone taking notes needs to pay attention not only to the content but also to the dynamics of the relationships created. This was what happened in the lively and spontaneous colloquium, lasting three hours, that the Holy Father granted to the Union of Superiors General (USG) of the male religious institutions at the end of their 82nd General Assembly on 29 November 2013.[1] Halfway through there was an interval of half an hour, in which the Pope took a break to talk to the Superiors General in person, also taking a cup of maté in a relaxed atmosphere.

In fact, the superiors had only requested a brief chance to greet the Pope, but Francis wanted to dedicate the whole morning to the colloquium. He decided not to deliver a speech, however, and not to listen to accounts that had already been prepared: he wanted a frank and free discussion, consisting of questions and answers.

It was 9.25, and the arrival of the photographers announced his imminent entry to the New Hall of the Synod in the Vatican, where some 120 superiors were waiting for him.

THE RELIGIOUS: SINNERS AND PROPHETS

Greeted by a round of applause, the Holy Father sat down at 9.30 precisely, looked at the clock and congratulated himself on his 'Swiss punctuality'. Everyone laughed: this was the Pope's way of greeting Fr Mauro Jöhri, the general minister of the Capuchin Friars Minor, a Swiss national who had just been elected vice-president of this Union.

After a brief word of greeting from the president, Fr Adolfo Nicolás, the general provost of the Jesuits, and the secretary-general, Fr David Glenday, a Comboni missionary, Pope Francis gave simple and cordial thanks for his invitation and immediately listened to a first group of questions. The generals focused their questions to the Pope on the identity and mission of the religious orders: 'What is expected of the consecrated life? What does it ask for? If you were in our place, how would you receive your appeal to go to the peripheries, to live the Gospel *sine glossa*, the evangelical prophecy? What would you feel called to do?' And 'Where should we place the emphasis today? What are the priorities?'

Pope Francis began by saying that he too is a member of a religious order and that he therefore knows from experience what is being talked about.[2] The last Pope to be a member of a religious order was the Camaldolese Gregory XVI, elected in 1831. Then he referred explicitly to Benedict XVI: 'He said that the Church grows through witness, not through proselytizing. The witness that can truly attract is the one who is bound to attitudes that are not the usual ones: generosity, detachment, sacrifice, forgetting oneself to attend to others. This is witness, the "martyrdom" of the religious life. And for the people it is an "alarm signal". The religious orders, through their lives, say to people: "What is happening?" These people are saying something to me! These people go beyond the worldly horizon! There it is,' the Pope went on, quoting Benedict XVI, 'the religious life must permit the growth of the Church through attraction.'[3]

So: 'The Church must be attractive. Wake up the world! Be witnesses to a different way of doing, of acting, of living! It is possible to live differently in this world. We are talking about an eschatological vision, the values of the Kingdom incarnated here, on this earth. It is a matter of leaving everything to follow the Lord. No, I don't mean being "radical". Evangelical radicalism is not just a matter for the religious orders: it is required of everyone. But the religious follow the Lord in a special way, a prophetic way. I expect that witness of you. The religious must be men and women who are capable of waking up the world.'

Pope Francis came back around in a circle to the concepts he had expressed, probing them progressively. He went on: 'You must be truly witnesses to a different way of acting and behaving. But in life it is difficult for everything to be clear, precise, clearly defined. Life is complex, it is made of grace and sin. If you don't sin, you are not human. We all make mistakes, and we must acknowledge our weakness. A religious who acknowledges that he is weak and a sinner does not contradict the witness he is called to give but reinforces it, and that is good for everyone. So what I expect is witness. I wish for that special testimony from the religious.'

AVOID FUNDAMENTALISM AND ILLUMINATE THE FUTURE

Continuing to answer the first questions, Pope Francis touched on one of the key points of his thought: 'I am convinced of one thing: the great changes of history come about when reality is seen not from the centre but from the periphery. It is a hermeneutic question: we can only understand reality if we look from the periphery, not if our gaze is placed at a centre equidistant from everything. To have a real understanding of reality, we must shift from the central position of calm and tranquillity and move ourselves towards the peripheral zone.[4] Being at the periphery helps us to see and understand more clearly, to have a more correct analysis of reality, rejecting centralism and ideological approaches.'

'So we should not be at the centre of a sphere. To understand, we must "displace" ourselves, see reality from several different points of view.[5] We have to get used to thinking. I often refer to a letter from Fr Pedro Arrupe, who was the general of the Society of Jesus. It was a letter addressed to the Centros de Investigación y Acción Social. In this letter Fr Arrupe spoke about poverty, and said that a period of real contact with the poor is a necessity. This is truly important for me: you need to know reality through experience, dedicate some time to going to the periphery to have a real knowledge of reality and people's lived experience. If this doesn't happen, you run the risk of being abstract ideologues or fundamentalists, and that isn't healthy.'[6]

Then the Pope paused on a concrete case, the apostolate to youth: 'If you work with young people, you can't say things that are too orderly, or structured like a treatise, because those things pass over the heads of boys and girls. We need a new language, a new way of saying things. Today God asks us this: to leave the nest that holds us in order to be sent out. Those who then live their consecration in seclusion experience that inner tension of prayer so that the Gospel can grow. The Gospel instruction to "Go into all the world and proclaim the Gospel to all creation" [Mk 16:15] can be accomplished with this hermeneutic key moved to existential and geographical peripheries. It is the most concrete way of imitating Jesus, who went towards every periphery. Jesus went towards everyone, really everyone. I wouldn't feel worried about going towards the periphery: don't be worried about approaching anyone.'

So, what is the priority of the consecrated life? The Pope replied: 'The prophecy of the Kingdom, which is not negotiable. The emphasis must be placed on being prophets, and not on playing at being them. Of course, the devil presents us with his temptations, and this is one of them: playing at being prophets without being prophets, assuming the attitudes. But you can't play with those things. I have seen many things that are very sad in that regard. No: religious are men and women who illuminate the future.' Pope Francis, in his interview with *La Civiltà Cattolica*, had clearly stated that religious are called to a prophetic life. This is their peculiarity: 'to be prophets who bear witness to how

Jesus lived on this earth, and who proclaim how the Kingdom of God will be in its perfection. A religious must never renounce prophecy. [...] Let us think about what the great monastic saints did, monks and nuns, from St Anthony Abbot onwards. Being prophets sometimes means making *ruido*, I don't know how to put it ... Prophecy makes a noise, it makes a racket, some people might say "trouble". But in fact its charism is about being leavened: prophecy proclaims the spirit of the Gospel.'[7]

So, how to be a prophet while living out one's own particularly religious charism? For Pope Francis it is important to 'reinforce what is institutional in consecrated life and not to confuse the institution with apostolic work. The first remains, the second passes.' The Pope goes on: 'Charism remains, it is strong, the work passes. Sometimes the institution becomes confused with the work. The institution is creative, it constantly seeks new ways. So the peripheries change, and you can always make a different list of them.'

'CHARISM IS NOT A BOTTLE OF DISTILLED WATER'

At this point the questions turned to the theme of vocations. A profound change is occurring in the human geography of the Church and hence of the religious institutions. Vocations are increasing in Africa and Asia, accounting now for the majority of the total number. All of this poses serious challenges: the inculturation of charism, vocational discernment and the selection of candidates, the challenge of inter-religious dialogue, the quest for a more equitable form of representation in the structure of the Church. So the Pope is asked to give some guidance about this situation.

Pope Francis says he is aware that a very great deal has changed in the geography of the consecrated life, and that 'all cultures have the capacity to be called by the Lord, who is free to prompt more vocations on one side or another. What does the Lord want with the vocations he is sending from the younger Churches? I don't know. But I ask myself that question. We need to ask it. The Lord's will is in all of this. There are Churches that are yielding new fruits. Perhaps they were once not so fruitful, but now they are. That naturally obliges us to rethink the inculturation of charism. Charism is one thing, but, as St Ignatius says, it must be lived out according to places, times and individuals. Charism is not a bottle of distilled water. It must be lived with energy, and culturally reread. But that way there is a risk of getting things wrong, you will say, of committing errors.

'It is risky. Of course it is: we will always make mistakes, there is no doubt about that. But that must not hold us back, because then there is a risk of making greater errors. In fact, we must always ask forgiveness and look with great shame at the apostolic failures caused by a lack of courage. Think, for example, of the pioneering intuitions of Matteo Ricci, which were rejected in his time.[8]

'I'm not talking about folkloristic adaptation to customs', the Pope went on. 'It's a question of mentality, of ways of thinking. For example, there are peoples who think in a way that is more concrete than abstract, or at least they have a kind of abstraction that is different from the Western one. I have seen that difference myself, as a Provincial of the Jesuits in Argentina. I remember how much trouble we had engaging in mutual dialogue, even about the simple things of daily life, with a Jesuit brother who came from the zone of the Guaraní, who have developed a very concrete way of thinking. You need to live with courage and face up to those challenges, even about important subjects. In short, I can't train a person as a religious without taking into account his life, his experience, his mentality and his cultural context. This is the path. This is what the great missionary religious have done. I think of the extraordinary adventures of the Spanish Jesuit Segundo Llorente, a tenacious and contemplative missionary in Alaska, who learned not only the language but also the concrete way of thinking of his people.[9] So inculturating charism is fundamental, and that never means relativizing it.

We must not make charism rigid and uniform. When we make our cultures uniform, we kill charism', the Pontiff concluded firmly, indicating the need to 'introduce into the central government of the Orders and Congregations individuals of different cultures, who express different ways of living charism'.

Pope Francis is certainly aware of the risks, even in terms of 'vocational recruitment' of the younger Churches. He recalled, among other things, that in 1994, in the context of the ordinary Synod on the consecrated life and his mission, the Filipino bishops denounced the 'trade in novices', meaning the massive influx of foreign congregations who opened houses on the archipelago with the aim of recruiting vocations to be transplanted to Europe. 'We need to have our eyes open about these situations', the Pope said.

Then he also addressed the issue of the vocation of brethren and, in more general terms, of religious who are not priests. He lamented the fact that no adequate awareness had developed about that specific vocation in the present day. He referred to a document on the subject that had never been published, and which might be taken up again and completed, and which might provide a more appropriate reflection on the subject. At this point the Pope looked towards Cardinal João Braz de Aviz, Prefect of the Congregation for the Institutes of Consecrated Life and the Societies of Apostolic Life, and the secretary of the same Congregation, Monsignor José Rodríguez Carballo, who were present in the assembly, inviting them to consider the question. He concluded: 'I do not in fact believe that the crisis in vocations of religious who are not priests is a sign of the times, telling us that that vocation is over. We must understand what God is asking of us.' Then, replying to a question on the issue of brother religious as superiors in clerical Orders, the Pope replied that this a canonical issue which must be confronted at that level.

'FORMATION MUST BE A WORK OF ART, NOT A POLICE ACTION'

Then Pope Francis listened to some questions on the subject of formation. He replied immediately, indicating priorities: 'The training of candidates is fundamental. There are four pillars of formation: spiritual, intellectual, community and apostolic. The fantasy that we need to combat is the image of the religious life seen as a consolation and a refuge from a difficult and complex "outside" world. The four pillars must interact from the first day of entering the novitiate, and they must not be structured in sequence. There must be interaction between them.'

The Pope is aware of the fact that the problem of formation today is not an easy one to confront: 'Today's culture is much richer and more conflict-ridden than it was years ago, in our day. Our culture was more simple and orderly. Today inculturation requires a different attitude. For example: problems cannot be resolved simply by forbidding people to do this or that. What we need is dialogue, and confrontation. To avoid problems, in some training houses, young people grit their teeth, try not to commit obvious errors, to stick to the rules while smiling all the time, waiting for someone to tell them one day, "Well, you've finished your training." This hypocrisy is the fruit of clericalism, which is one of the most terrible evils. I said to the bishops of the Latin American Episcopal Conference (CELAM) in Rio de Janeiro this summer: we need to overcome that tendency towards clericalism, not least in training houses and seminaries. I sum it up in some advice that I was once given as a young man: "If you want to advance, think clearly and speak obscurely." It was a clear invitation to hypocrisy. It has to be avoided at all costs.' In Rio, in fact, the Pope had identified clericalism as one of the causes of the 'lack of maturity and Christian freedom' of the people of God.[10]

So, 'if the seminary is too big, it must be divided into communities with trainers who are really capable of following people. The dialogue must be serious, without fear, sincere. And we must bear in mind that the language of young people in training today is different from the one that came before: we are living through a change of eras. Formation must be a work of art, not a police action. We must form hearts. Otherwise we are forming little monsters. And then those little monsters form the people of God. That really gives me goose bumps.' Then the Pope stressed the fact that training must be oriented not only towards personal growth but also towards the final goal: the people of God. When training people, we must think of those to whom they will be sent: 'We must always think of the faithful, of the faithful people of God. We must train people who are witnesses to the resurrection of Jesus. The trainer must bear in mind that the person being trained will be called to heal the people of God. We must always think of the people of God, inside the people. Think of those religious whose hearts are as sour as vinegar: they are not made for the people. To sum up: we must train not administrators, managers, but fathers, brothers, travelling companions.'

Finally, Pope Francis wanted to give an example of another risk: 'If a young man who has been invited to leave a religious Institute, because of problems of training and for serious reasons, is then accepted into a seminary, this is another big problem. I'm not talking about people who acknowledge that they are sinners: we are all sinners, but we are not all corrupt. Sinners may be accepted, but not the corrupt.' And here the Pope recalled the big decision made by Benedict XVI in confronting cases of abuse: 'This should serve as an example to us of the need to have the courage to assume personal training as a serious challenge, always having in mind the people of God.'

LIVING BROTHERHOOD 'BY EMBRACING CONFLICT'

The Synod on the New Evangelization had asked religious to be witnesses to the humanizing strength of the Gospel through the fraternal life. On the basis of this appeal, the Pope was asked some questions about the fraternal life of religious: 'How do we keep together the commitments of mission and those of community life? How do we fight the tendency towards individualism? How do we behave with brothers who are in difficulty, or who are experiencing or creating conflicts? How do we combine the right answer with mercy when faced with difficult cases?'

Pope Francis recalled that the previous day he had received a visit from the prior of Taizé, Brother Alois: 'At Taizé there are Catholic monks, Calvinists, Lutherans ... all truly living a life of brotherhood. They are an impressive apostolic centre for young people. Brotherhood has a huge force of convocation. The illnesses of brotherhood, on the other hand, have a destructive force. The temptation against brotherhood is the biggest impediment to a path into the consecrated life. Basically the individualist tendency is a way of not enduring brotherhood. St John Berchmans said that for him the greatest penitence was community life itself.[11] Sometimes it is hard to lead a life of brotherhood, but if you don't lead that life, you are not fruitful. Work, even "apostolic" work, can become an escape from the fraternal life. If a person cannot lead a life of fraternity, they cannot lead a religious life.

'Religious fraternity,' the Pope went on, 'with all its possible differences, is an experience of love that goes beyond conflicts. Community conflicts are inevitable: in a sense they have to exist, if the community really leads a life of sincere and loyal relationships. This is life. To think of a community without brothers living in difficulties makes no sense, and does no good. If a community does not suffer conflicts, it means that something is missing. Reality tells us that in all families and in all human groups there is conflict. And conflict must be confronted head on: it must not be ignored. If it is covered up, it creates pressure and then explodes. A life without conflicts is not a life.'

The values at stake are high. We know that one of Pope Francis's fundamental principles is that 'unity is superior to conflict'. His words to the religious should be read in the light of *Evangelii gaudium* (nos 226–230), where he asks us to be 'willing to face conflict head on, to resolve it and to make it a link in the chain of a new process' (no. 227). We must recall that for Bergoglio personal realization is never an exclusively individual enterprise but always a collective, community one.[12] In this sense conflict can, indeed must, evolve in a process of ripening.

In any case, however, conflict needs company: 'We must never behave like the priest or the Levite in the parable of the Good Samaritan, who simply walk past. But how do we do that? I think', the Pope says, 'of the story of a young man of 22 who was in a deep depressive crisis. I'm not speaking about a religious, but a young man who lived with his mother, who was a widow and washed clothes for a well-to-do family. This young man stopped going to work and lived in a fog of alcohol. There was nothing his mother could do, except that every morning before she went out she looked at him with great tenderness. This young man is now an important person: he overcame that crisis, because in the end his mother's tender gaze gave him a shaking up. So you see we have to recapture that tenderness, not least maternal tenderness. Think of the tenderness that St Francis experienced, for example. Tenderness helps us through conflicts. And if that's not enough, one may also need to change communities.

'It's true,' Pope Francis went on, 'sometimes we are very cruel. We experience the common temptation to criticize for personal satisfaction or to provoke a personal advantage. Sometimes crises of fraternity are due to the fragility of the individual, and in that case it is necessary to request the help of a professional, a psychologist. We must not be afraid of that; we must not fear falling inevitably into psychologism. But we must never, ever act as managers when faced with a brother's conflict. We must involve the heart.

'Fraternity is a very delicate matter. In the first hymn in the liturgy of the hours of the solemnity of St Joseph in the Argentine breviary, the saint is asked to guard the Church with *ternura de eucaristía*, "Eucharistic tenderness".[13] That's how we should treat our brethren: with Eucharistic tenderness. We must embrace conflict. I remember when Paul VI received a letter from a child with lots of drawings. Pope Paul said that, on a table covered with newly arrived letters about problems, the arrival of a letter like that did him a lot of good. Tenderness does us good. Eucharistic tenderness doesn't cover over conflict, but helps us face it as human beings.'

THE MUTUAL RELATIONS BETWEEN RELIGIOUS AND LOCAL CHURCHES

At this point the Superiors General asked the Pope some questions about the place of religious communities in local Churches, and about relations with bishops. How can the charisms of the various Institutes be respected and promoted for the good of the local Church? How do we promote communion among the different charisms and the forms of Christian life for the greatest growth of all, and to encourage better development of the mission?

Pope Francis replied that for many years there has been a request pending to revise the directive criteria concerning the relationships between bishops and religious in the Church that arose in 1978 from the Congregation for Religious and the Congregation for Bishops (*Mutuae relationes*). The Pope is of the opinion that the time is ripe because 'that document was responding to a certain time and is no longer current. The charisms of the various Institutes need to be respected and promoted because they are needed in the dioceses. I know from experience', he went on, 'the problems that can arise between the bishop and the religious communities.' For example: 'If they decide one day to abandon a project for lack of religious, the bishop often finds himself holding a hot potato. I've had difficult experiences in that respect. I was told that the work was about to be abandoned and I didn't know what to do. Once they actually presented it to me as a *fait accompli*. But I could also tell you of many very positive episodes. In short: I know the problems, but I also know that the bishops don't always know the charisms and the works of the religious. We bishops need to understand that consecrated people aren't just a material help; they are charisms that enrich the dioceses. The diocesan involvement of religious communities is important. We need to rescue dialogue between bishop and religious to ensure that, without an understanding of charisms, bishops don't just use religious as handy tools.' So the Pope has given the Congregation for Religious the task of resuming reflection and working on a revision of the document *Mutuae relationes*.

THE FRONTIERS OF MISSION: MARGINALIZATION, CULTURE AND EDUCATION

The last questions concerned the frontiers of the mission of the consecrated. The Pope has often spoken of 'going out', of 'leaving', of 'frontiers'. So the Superiors General asked which frontiers they should go out towards: 'How do you see the presence of the consecrated life in the realities of exclusion that exist in our world? Many institutions perform an educational role: how do you see that kind of service? What would you say to religious who are involved in that field?'

First of all, the Pope stated that of course there are still geographical frontiers, and that we must be potentially mobile. But there are also symbolic frontiers, which are not pre-established and not the same for everybody, but which 'should be sought according to the charisms of each Institute. So everything must be discerned according to the charism in question. Certainly, the realities of exclusion remain the most significant priorities, but they require discernment. The first criterion in those situations of exclusion and marginalization is to send the best, the most gifted people. There are situations of greater risk that call for courage and a lot of prayer. And the superior needs to accompany the people who are involved in that work.' There is always a risk, the Pope reminded his interlocutors, of becoming over-enthusiastic, of sending to those frontiers religious who were well intentioned but not a match for the situation. Decisions should not be taken about the marginalized without the assurance offered by discernment and support.

For the Pope, the pillars of education are 'To transmit knowledge, to transmit ways of doing things, to transmit values. It is through these that faith is transmitted. The educator must have an understanding of the people he is educating, he must think about how to proclaim Jesus Christ to a changing generation.' Then he went on: 'The educational task is a key mission today, it is key, it is key!' And he cited some of his experiences in Buenos Aires highlighting the preparation required to welcome into educational contexts children and young people who live in complex situations, especially in the family: 'I remember the case of a very sad little girl who eventually told the teacher the reason for her state of mind: "My mother's boyfriend doesn't like me." The percentage of children studying at the school with separated parents is extremely high. So the situations we are experiencing today present new challenges that are sometimes difficult even for us to understand. How to proclaim Christ to these children? How to proclaim Christ to a changing generation? You have to be careful not to inoculate them against faith.'[14]

———

At the end of the three hours, at about 12.30, the Pope said he was sorry to have to close the conversation: 'Let us leave other questions for the next time', he said with a smile. He confided in us that the dentist was waiting for him. Before saying goodbye to the Superiors General, he had an announcement to make: 2015 would be a year dedicated to the consecrated life. These words were welcomed with lengthy applause. The Pope smiled at the prefect and the secretary of the Congregation for Religious and the Secular Institutes, saying, 'It's their fault, it's a suggestion of theirs: when those two meet, they're dangerous', provoking great hilarity among the whole assembly.

Leaving the hall, he said: 'Thank you, thank you for the act of faith that you performed at this meeting. Thank you for what you are doing, for your spirit of faith and your quest for service. Thanks for your testimony, for the acts of witness that you constantly give to the Church, and also for the humiliations through which you must pass: it is the way of the Cross. My heartfelt thanks.'

2

GO OUT TO THE PERIPHERIES OF EXISTENCE: A DIALOGUE WITH THE FILIPINO JESUITS

Pope Francis's meeting with the Filipino Jesuits took place at 7.30 p.m. on 16 January 2015. The Pontiff had landed in Manila the previous day, at about 6.00 p.m. On that day, a Friday, he met the president, the civil authorities and the diplomatic corps. Then he celebrated Mass with the bishops, priests and religious. In the afternoon he had gone to the Mall of Asia arena to meet families. After an intense day he wanted to meet the Jesuits in the Manila Nunciature, his place of residency. There were 40 of them, chosen according to various stages of their training. With them was the Provincial, Fr Tony Moreno. Also present were Fr Federico Lombardi and Fr Antonio Spadaro.

Entering the meeting room, the Pope greeted them one by one and then sat down at a table, with all the others seated around him. He greeted them all, saying that he would speak in Spanish and that he had not prepared anything, but was prepared to answer any questions. And suddenly a hand went up ...

———

The Jesuit Fr Louis Catalan rose to his feet to speak, but the Pope gestured to him to sit down: he wanted this to be a chat in a relaxed atmosphere. 'What's your impression of the Filipinos?' Fr Catalan asked.

'There was a Jesuit in Argentina who was dedicated to the intellectual apostolate, and he was invited to various parts of the world to give lectures. He stayed for a week in each country he travelled to. On his return he wrote a book about the social, political and religious reality of that country. And he sold those books! Well, I don't want to do that with my journey!

'But there is one thing that I want to say. I've seen many Filipinos working not in Argentina but in Rome. I've found something in you that I can't put my finger on, but which gives you dignity. For example, where I live, in Casa Santa Marta, there are workers who come from the Philippines. You have something special inside you. A root ... When those people speak, they talk about their parents and grandparents, I notice a special rootedness in the fourth commandment. In short, that is what I've seen: dignity.

'Here I see enthusiasm. Overflowing enthusiasm. They show me their children when I pass: for me, that is a promise of the future. And I have also been struck by devotion to the rosary. You Filipinos are very devoted to the Virgin, to the rosary.'

Fr Tony Moreno, the Provincial, asked the second question, but he began with a joke, saying that in Sri Lanka the Pope had been welcomed by 40 elephants, and in the Philippines by 40 Jesuits. Francis confirmed this, but he added 'But the elephants were better dressed!', causing much hilarity. Then Fr Moreno went on, asking: 'What is your message for the Filipino Jesuits?'

'Two things: the first is to go to the peripheries. This is the identity and the charism of the Jesuits. If a Jesuit forgets to go to the peripheries, he has lost as badly as if he had lost a war. He will find other resources, but he lacks what St Ignatius wanted the Jesuits to show before the Lord: discernment. We must go out to the peripheries of existence. To some, the address by the Blessed Paul VI to the 32nd General Congregation seemed like a challenge, but in fact it was an exhortation to go out to the peripheries. I would suggest that you reread it in these terms: go out to the peripheries! Throughout history the Jesuits have always been at a historical crossroads.

'But we must address both sorts of peripheries, the physical and the spiritual. I have lived very closely with Fr Arrupe. Arrupe's actions have always touched me a great deal. He was a prophet to me: he had an intuitive sense of commitment to refugees. And his swan-song, as he called it, was the foundation in Bangkok of the Jesuit service for refugees. Then at night, on the flight to Rome from Thailand, he had a stroke. And the speech that he had given to the Jesuits who were working with refugees was about not neglecting prayer. Which is to say: when you are on that physical periphery, do not forget the other, spiritual one.

'He who was to be brought down by a stroke only a few hours later, rendering him unable to govern, said, "This is my swan-song." An impressive and truly prophetic thing. And to think that he had taken on a Society of Jesus that had become a little sleepy, and dragged it out of its inertia. I remember an anecdote about Fr Ledóchowski: he was a high-ranking man in the government of the Church, but he thought he would help the Society by imposing the *Epitome Instituti*, disciplining everyone.[1] Satisfied, he took it to the first abbot of the Benedictines, who thanked him very much. But a few days later he called him back and said, "With this text you have killed the Society." A static Society, full of missionaries all over the place, but with a dogma of disciplinary government. When I joined the novitiate in 1958, everything was regulated according to the customs of the novitiate of Villagarcía. On Sunday, when I had listened to the sermon, I didn't examine my conscience. If St Ignatius had had them within reach, he would have given them a good scolding: the customs were making them lose the very essence. The examination of conscience is essential for discernment. When I listened to the sermon, there was no examination of conscience ... so the Society had disciplined itself statically.

'After the war Fr Janssens tried to make that change, but by then everything was stuck in a rut. But then the Society, by the grace of God, elected Arrupe, a prophet. Yes, of course, some of my neighbours across the corridor where I live will say that he was a progressive, a communist; he was slandered a lot by many people in the Roman Curia. But he also had many good friends. Yet many in the Church slandered him because he wanted to revive and reinvigorate the Society. Among the first things he did were to open a centre of spirituality and promote the journal *Christus* ... He launched a strategy ... That is our recent history.

'Perhaps I'm digressing, but to understand the fact of the two peripheries we need to look at that model. Then in Spain there was the movement of the "true Jesuits", the ones someone called the "barefoot Jesuits", who wanted to take everything backwards and erase Arrupe's work. But Arrupe was a man of obedience. He didn't take a step without the permission of the Pope, or at least the authorization of the Pope, or without the Pope being aware of it. And we must thank God for the fact that he helped us to find that path through many centres of spirituality.'

At this point the Provincial wanted to give the Pope two gifts: a replica of the statue of the Sacred Heart made by José Rizal and a CD of music entitled *Mercy and Compassion: Songs for Pope Francis*. This was followed by questions from Fr Jett Villarin: 'What does it feel like to be Pope? And what is your relationship with the Society now?'

'I don't mind being Pope. Fr Spadaro knows that, you can talk to him about it! The election was an unexpected thing: it came out of the blue and took away my peace of mind. And ... I'm very happy about it. Why should I pretend and say "Poor me ..."? I took it as something quite natural from God. But when I'm with people, I'm happy. For example, this morning, while I was with people, when I went to see the children at the orphanage. I was also very happy when I was a parish priest, because when I was rector of the Collegio Massimo I was also parish priest of the local parish, and the parish always made me extremely happy. I take it quite naturally ... I am content. And as to the Society, I am a good friend of the Father General; we talk very often on the telephone. The other day I went to lunch with the community of the Curia, I met Jesuits like Fr Spadaro from *La Civiltà Cattolica* and others too.

'You will have heard that I've been through a very difficult time in the life of the Society. Gossip is flying around. But that very fact helps to confer a certain maturity: above all, maturity doesn't blame anyone, it means just accepting your own responsibility. That helps you to mature and lets you see things differently. If you say to me: "Are you reconciled with the Society?" I reply: "No. Because I've never argued with them." I really haven't. There are different points of view, misunderstandings and nothing else, but they helped to purify: to purify the communities, to purify me, to purify false expectations.'

After that question Fr Mark Raper, president of the Conference of Jesuit Provincials in the Asia-Pacific area, raised his hand and pointed to a Jesuit from China, Joseph. The Chinese Jesuit stepped forward and knelt in front of the Pope, taking some rosaries from his pocket to have them blessed. 'I come from China. Will you come to visit us?' he said. And the Pope replied with joy: 'I want to go, yes, I want to go there!' And this was followed by emotional applause. Next, Fr Bienvenido Nebres passed on to the Pope a message from the young people of Tacloban. Then Fr Florge Sy asked a question: 'How are you? How do you take care of your health?'

'My Franciscan confessor often gives me some instructions as to how to look after my health, but I don't follow his advice!'

Then Fr Xavier Olin spoke to the Pope about young people and asked: 'There are 900 young people gathered together at the Ignatian Youth Camp. Do you have a message for them?'

'My message for them is not to be afraid. A frightened young person is an old person. Don't be afraid to be imprudent. You will always be imprudent. Don't be afraid to come forward for the challenges that you will encounter in life: embrace them! Don't be afraid of walking with people, with other men and women ... Walk with Christ! But don't walk on your own!'

Fr Frank Savadera stayed on the topic of young people, but thinking about vocational promotion: 'How should vocations be accompanied?'

'Above all, we must be honest in answering the questions that young people can ask us. And also, we have to accompany the candidates. One at a time. We have to accompany their process. A vocational process requires patience. A young person comes and goes. You have to have a lot of patience. No one who undertakes a life following Jesus does it with 100 per cent pure intentions: it is always mixed up with other things, and they need to be purified along the way. There is no such thing as a pure-bred Jesuit: and if such a person doesn't exist at the end, you can imagine what it's like at the start. You will find no one who is perfect. Prepare to accompany them.'

Fr Chester Yacub, hospital chaplain, asked a question on behalf of the ill: 'Can you give us a message for the sick?'

'I tell you that you must treat them with affection: they are the flesh of Christ, and the message is that Jesus is always close to them, Jesus sees himself reflected in the mirror of those who suffer. And when he sees them, he sees himself, he finds himself in them. Trust in that reality, which is not a pious little tale of devotees but a theological truth. When Jesus sees someone who is suffering, he sees himself in them. In fact, Jesus isn't just partying in heaven. In the Epistle to the Hebrews he is said to be interceding, showing the Father his wounds, and his wounds are the faces of the suffering, in which he sees himself. It is not a pious little tale; it is the pure and real and up-to-date truth of our supreme priest, Jesus. Tell him, make him hear. It gives a great deal of consolation.'

Fr Archie Carampatan, who works with migrants, asked: 'Do you have a message to give to refugees?'

'The migrant is passing through the Stations of the Cross. The worst thing that can happen to him is that he ends up becoming a slave worker. And then there is the abuse and all the things that can happen ... When I went to Lampedusa, a young Eritrean told me that from the moment when he fled his country to come to Europe in search of a future three years passed, and in those three years he had been kidnapped and made into a slave, he had suffered sexual abuse five times. Once he had been sold as a slave. The things they go through are terrible. And then, once they are here, they are faced with contempt. In Argentina, many immigrants from Bolivia and Paraguay had their passports taken away so that they couldn't return home, and at that point they were exploited. The life of refugees is a *via crucis*. So Arrupe had that prophetic vision. This emergency apostolate must be taken on by the Society, by the Church.'

At about 8.20 the organizers of the trip gestured to the Pope to tell him that it was time to leave. So Fr Joel Tabora asked the Pope for a blessing. Then came the moment of the group photograph. A novice, Harold, spontaneously asked for a hug, and was given one. Then, after the hymn 'Amare et servire', composed by the Jesuit Manuel Francisco, the Pope withdrew, saying:

'Thank you for this meeting, and please don't forget to pray for me. I need it.'

3

A Shepherd's Footsteps:
A conversation with Antonio Spadaro

It is the morning of 9 July 2016. I arrive early, but the porter's office tells me to go up without waiting. On the second floor I find that the door is already open.

Before the trip to Armenia I told the Pope that I intended to publish all of his homilies and sermons as archbishop of Buenos Aires. I had had that project in mind for a long time. In those writings I found a spiritual and pastoral depth that couldn't be left in the drawer or brought out in themed anthologies. The important thing was to present the flow of his pastoral inspiration, his lived experience in contact with the people of God. It was also a matter of showing the maternal womb of the Church in which Francis's Petrine ministry had been shaped over time. The publisher had decided to bring the project forward. And I talked to the Pope about that, also asking him to get involved with this volume. He told me he would think about it.

On the flight back from Yerevan, after a very intense trip, the Pope called me to come and sit beside him for a while. We talked about various things, and then he started discussing the book of homilies again. He told me he had thought about it and, yes, he approved of that collection and agreed to make himself available for a colloquium which would then be transcribed. He preferred a conversation to a more traditional preface. He found it more 'alive'. I had the distinct impression that his 'yes' was not merely a 'concession' but a precise decision. He had had a spiritual discernment. That's how he takes his decisions. In any case, our past contains living traces of the passage of God. Those homilies today are a profound trace of that passage. They say something to the present day.

I didn't know how to prepare for this interview. I was convinced that I should concentrate not on the subjects addressed in sermons but on the deeper significance of preaching, on the very experience of preaching as the experience of a rich and complex life. I had prepared some questions, but without being concerned about having to find answers to all of them. I would let the conversation and the memories flow. But I had done some preparation by talking to his Jesuit confrères who knew him in his Argentine years.

The Pope invites me to sit down wherever I like. I choose the usual armchair from my previous conversations. I notice that its left arm is already quite worn.

The Pope sits down on the sofa to my left. I feel surrounded by the pictures that hang on the walls and embrace the room: two mosaics by Fr Marko Rupnik – a Madonna and Child, St Joseph sleeping with an angel whispering something in his ear – and then, on the opposite side, an icon of St Francis and St Dominic and, above it, an icon of Moses by the burning bush. Pope Francis tells me they were given to him by some nuns from Syria. And in front of that icon he prays and always remembers the Middle East. On a small table there is a statuette of the Madonna of Luján. I know that in the conversation I will have to ask him about the sanctuary of Luján.

We start talking about various things. I show him the last issue of *Civiltà Cattolica*, and we talk about it. Then the conversation flows naturally and directly around the subject of the meeting.

———

LOOKING PEOPLE IN THE EYE

'Do you remember your first homily as a priest? What did you talk about? What were your feelings?' I ask him. I'm expecting an in-depth answer, and instead the Pope tells me he doesn't remember. And he adds: 'Generally speaking, I don't really remember past homilies. For me the homily is so bound up with the concrete history of the moment that it can be forgotten afterwards. It isn't made to be remembered by the preacher, who is always driven forwards.'

His statement surprises me because I know that he has an excellent memory, but I understand there is a spiritual element here that makes me think. I thought it might be linked at least to some particularly effective homily, or delivered on a special occasion. And instead I understand that he's remote from this kind of petty narcissism. If his words are useful, he is glad that people remember and meditate on them. But he has already moved on.

And yet he adds a memory from before his ordination as a priest: 'When they taught us homiletics in the seminary, I already felt a strong aversion to written pages that contained everything. I remember that very clearly. I was and remain convinced that there should be nothing between the preacher and the people of God. There shouldn't be a piece of paper. A written note, yes, but not more than that. And I said that, at school, back then. The professor was startled. He asked me why I was so opposed to the idea of preparing the whole homily. And I replied: "If you are reading it, you can't look people in the eye." I remember it as clearly as if it were today. And it happened before I was ordained.

'That's the point: the true problem of the written homily is that it distracts you from looking at the people you're preaching to. What I'm trying to do is find people's eyes. Even here in St Peter's Square.'

I ask the Pope how he looks people in the eye when there are so many of them in such a big square.

'Yes', he says. 'When I greet them, there's a crowd. But I don't see them as a crowd: I try to look at least at one person, one particular face. Sometimes it's actually impossible because of the distance. It's difficult when they're too far away. Sometimes I don't succeed, but I try. If I succeed, I see that there's something, that something happens. If I look at someone, perhaps other people feel looked at as well. Not as a "crowd", but as individuals, as people. I look at individuals, and they all feel looked at. In the Philippines, for example, the homily of the last Mass in front of millions of people may not have been as warm as I would have liked. I love those people so much, and there were so many of them. In Tacloban, on the other hand, in the rain, in that really difficult situation, I felt that I could look at people and talk straight to their hearts. It was a direct communication. So, situations are unpredictable; communication is a thing that happens at the moment when it happens.'

'Of course,' I say to him, 'now you always have a finished text in front of you, except here in Casa Santa Marta, where you preach without notes.'

'Yes, now obviously I often have to read my homilies', he replies. 'And then I remember what I said as a student. That's why I so often stray from the prepared written text. I add words and expressions that aren't written down. That way I look at people. When I speak, I have to speak to someone. I do what I can, but I have this deep need. It's true that at St Peter's you have to go with something well prepared. But I always have this deep need which goes beyond formal contexts. Sometimes circumstances mean that I don't succeed, and then I'm not happy. I have this impulse to leave the written text, to look people in the eye.'

As he says these words, I see the Pope moving, and in the movements of his hand and the expression on his face I see the desire he is talking to me about. It's as if he wants to make me 'see' and not just 'say'. At that point I understand how difficult it is for him to stay inside a text. The homily isn't a text; it's a situation that produces language. Previous study, the preparation of the text, is no substitute for that original movement of contact with people. The Church going out also means leaving the rigidity of a product of reflection.

'On your travels sometimes you need to be translated. What do you feel about the need to be translated? Do you feel unease, detachment? Or do you feel that the message is getting there, that it "works?"' I ask him. He replies: 'I would rather not be translated, but speak the language. But I've got used to it. For example, Monsignor Mark Miles translates me well. He translates almost simultaneously.'

I ask him: 'In your writings, and in your homilies from the time of the Society, one notices a richness, a creativity and an audacity. How did you preach in those days? Is there a difference between your preaching as a Jesuit, as an archbishop and as the Pope?'

'I don't know', he says, perplexed and not very interested by the question. 'No, I'm not aware of a difference. Certainly in some cases as an archbishop and as the Pope sometimes the preparation is more formal and complex.'

'Very often you use a three-point structure. Why the three-idea or three-point structure rather than developing a theme?' I ask him.

'It comes from the *Exercises of St Ignatius*: it is the Jesuit training', he replies.

'But the Ignatian spirituality that trained you as a Jesuit helps you to construct the framework of your sermons?' I press.

'Always,' he replies. 'The *Exercises* always come into my mind, always. They shaped me. But since then, since the outset, I don't notice a radically different attitude from when I preached as a parish priest. The important thing is to have the heart of the pastor, whether as a parish priest, a bishop or a Pope.'

'Are there particular preachers who are dear to you?' I ask him.

'Yes, many parish priests, in fact.'

BEING THE ANGEL

'What is the difference between a homily and a lecture?' I ask him.

'The homily is the proclamation of the Word of God; the lecture is the explanation of the Word of God. The homily is the proclamation, it's being the angel. The lecture is being the doctor of the Church.'

I go on: 'What does the homily mean for you? What is the right attitude that the pastor needs to have?'

'It's all bound up with being a pastor, with the people who are in the community and listening. And it is also bound up with the pastor's prayer and the Word of God. If those things are missing, it's not a homily', the Pope replies.

'And then,' I go on, 'how do you prepare the homilies in Santa Marta? Where do those words come from?'

'I start the day before. At midday the previous day. I read the texts the day afterwards, in general, I choose one of the two readings. Then I read aloud the passage that I've chosen. I need to understand the sound, to listen to the words. And then in the little book I use I underline the ones that strike me the most. I make little circles around the words that strike me. Then for the rest of the day the words and thoughts come and go while I do what I have to do: I meditate, reflect, enjoy things ... But there are days when I come home in the evening and nothing comes to mind, when I have no idea what I'm going to say the next day. Then I do what St Ignatius says to do: I sleep on it. And then all of a sudden, when I wake up, inspiration comes. The right things come, sometimes strong, sometimes not so strong. But that's how it is: I feel ready.'

The Pope tells me that speaking without the text in front of him doesn't mean not preparing himself. Quite the opposite. In fact, a short homily requires a spiritual preparation, a preparation of discernment that can take a whole day.

I don't give up, and instead go back to the past, trying to make the Pope talk about his personal experience, his time in Buenos Aires.

'Do you remember one particular homily among so many?' I ask him.

The Pope insists he doesn't remember so spontaneously. But I see that he's struggling to remember something, because the memories are clearly stored somewhere, but it's as if he doesn't give them any particular relevance. Closing his eyes tightly as if to squeeze out the memories, he tells me he remembers a homily for the 50th anniversary of the priesthood of Cardinal Quarracino.[1] He tells me it was particularly solemn, for Corpus Christi, with a lot of people in the square.

I start again, talking about Luján. I tell the Pope that I was there and talk to him about my memories, about the Mass I celebrated there. I tell him I went to the church of San Gaetano, where he used to celebrate the saint's feast day for the many people who came to him for work and bread. I also talk to him about the *villas miseria* where I went with Fr Pepe Di Paola.[2] I say to him: 'I imagined you there, with the people, preaching. Did it go well? How? Were you at your ease, preaching to people?'

He says: 'Preaching has always done me good, always. It has always made me happy. What would make me unhappy would be if I had to deliver a funeral sermon giving a eulogy for the dead. I always try to aim for the Word of God, to talk about that. If I have to do more than that, I do it before the final blessing.'

But then he drops the topic of funerals, even though with his words he has given me to understand that the centrality of the Word of God is irreplaceable in preaching, whatever the situation.

'Let's get back to people', he goes on, brightening at the memory of the situation. 'In Luján, during the pilgrimage, when two million people arrive in two days, preaching was done early in the morning. I was preaching at seven in the morning, and that Mass was full of people. And I celebrated it after taking confession at night. I took confession from six till ten in the evening. Then I went and had a bite to eat. I slept for a while, and then at one in the morning I went back to church and took confession until six. Then

Mass. Sometimes I didn't manage to pray 200 rosaries because there wasn't time: the queue of people was sometimes uninterrupted. And there were 30 of us confessors in the basilica! I listened to people telling their life experiences. That prepares you for preaching: listening to people's lives. If you don't listen to people, how are you going to preach?'

I can see that he's concentrating once again, as if to gaze into his memories.

'I remember there was once a young man. I saw him walking back and forth, here and there as I was taking confession ... he looked away, he came over and he asked me: "What's happening here?" I said to him, "I'm taking confessions." And I asked him, "Have you never confessed?" "Yes," he said to me, "when I took my first communion, but I don't remember." And he started talking, talking, talking ... and so he confessed! Obviously my encounter with that young man featured in my homily of the day: I couldn't act as if I hadn't met him. He had touched my soul. Those are the experiences that fill your heart and help you to preach!'

Then the Pope stares into the distance and remembers another experience. Again, as if he were staring at a face. And he talks to me about this. He starts moving and imitating a man, describing his long hair, describing him from head to hips with a hand gesture. He also imitates the hard expression on his face. I had never seen Francis so theatrical, with so keen a desire to act out the characters who emerge so vividly from his memory.

'He was a big lad', he says, with a gesture to show his biceps. I feel like laughing when I see him imitating the person like that, but I also understand that his description is serious and full of affection. He says: 'He was about 23, with ear-rings. He sat down and said to me: "I've come in search of an answer because I have a problem, a problem that's troubling me." And he told me the problem. He couldn't cope any longer. "My mother," he went on, "is on her own, she brought me up as a single mother, and she works as a maid. I studied at technical college, and I'm a skilled worker."

'He wasn't married', the Pope explains, 'and he didn't mention any kind of girlfriend or fiancée. The problem was different: "One day," he goes on, "I couldn't cope any longer and I said to my mother: I've got this problem. My mother told me to come and see the Madonna in Luján because she would tell me what to do. And before coming here I went and stood in front of the Madonna and I heard that I had to do this and this and this ... Now I'm confessing ..." And he opened his heart. There, you see', the Pope says to me, 'the day after, how are you going to ignore the fact that you met this boy? I couldn't. I couldn't ignore him emotionally.

'What am I trying to tell you? That the closer you are to people, the better you preach, or the closer you bring the Word of God to their lives. So you link the Word of God with a human experience that needs that Word. The further you get from people and their problems, the more you take refuge in a limited theology of "You have to do this and not that", which communicates nothing, which is empty, abstract, lost in the void, in thoughts ... Sometimes with our words we answer questions that no one is asking.'

I realize that the Pope has warmed up as he tells me this, that he's talking to me from the heart.

'I have a nephew who goes to Mass with his family every Sunday. They have two parishes near by, but they don't lead a parochial life. They meet up with Catholic friends, but without belonging to groups. In one parish there's a priest who preaches well. In another there's a priest who delivers theological lessons. And if he's been to see the parish priest who gives the lessons, he tells me what theologian he talked about. You see, that's what's happening in our churches. But the people bring you close to reality. The Lord spoke like that, in contact with people. The Lord's homilies are direct and concrete: he talked about the things that the peasants and shepherds knew from experience. He didn't talk about abstract concepts.'

'And what were the homilies like in Luján?' I ask him.

'Well, in Luján, after a night of pilgrimage and vigil, you couldn't deliver a long and abstract sermon. People were tired, they were sleeping on the floor in the sanctuary. The sermon had to be … pared down.'

And here the Pope imitates the gesture of a pointed blade cutting and piercing. As he does so, he leaps up from the sofa. It couldn't be more dramatic. He repeats the hand gesture three times with the intensity of an actor.

'The sermon must be a pep talk. That was at Luján. In San Gaetano it wasn't so tiring, but it was tiring afterwards when, wearing all my robes, I went to the door of the church to greet the people who were arriving and leaving. Sometimes saying hello and goodbye took two hours. Once a woman said to me, "Father, I have sinned!" And I said straight away, "Confess!" And she says, "I've got seven children and I haven't baptized any of them." And I said, "Why?" And she says, "They told me I had to keep it." And I said, "How old is the eldest?" And she says, "Nineteen." So I told her to call me. She called me, and we reached an agreement. I told her what to teach her children, what prayers, I explained to her how to prepare them. She knew the prayers, the catechism. I understood that she was doing the preparation. And then I baptized all seven of them at the Curia. At San Gaetano the homily was for that precise historical moment, for the workers, to ask the saint for bread and work. I did a lot of preparation for that. It was really important.'

BURNING THE DEVIL

'But before being archbishop you were parish priest at the Istituto Massimo. What do you remember of that time? What was it like being a parish priest?' I ask him.

'I was rector of the faculty at the Collegio Massimo, and I was also parish priest there. So I was rector of the Jesuit students, the "scholastics", and I was also parish priest. I did both things at the same time. That was why I asked the Jesuits in training to carry on the work. I gave the instructions. The parish was full of children. The students went out to find children in every corner of the area, and they turned up in huge numbers. They came to the Collegio Massimo, which has very big spaces, and played. I always said Mass for the children, and on Saturday I taught catechism. Not every week, because I couldn't, but often. That was how I fulfilled the vow that St Ignatius makes professed Jesuits take to teach children.'

At this point the Pope begins to remember, and smiles. He says to me: 'The children's Mass was the most beautiful thing. I remember the first Sunday in Lent. There were more than 300 children ...'

At this point the Pope imitates what he did with them, even the tone of voice, guiding but affectionate: 'You be quiet … and you, you, come here …'. 'And then a real theatre began!' he says to me. 'I played a part. I preached like this. For example, on the first Sunday in Lent I asked: "What did the devil do with Jesus? He did that because he wanted Jesus to submit … he, the devil, wanted to rule…" "Do you understand what the devil is?" I once asked very heatedly. And the children, in the grip of emotion, shouted out loud with words and sounds to show that they knew very well, how bad he was, and how he should be kept far away.

'"And be careful, children," I said to the children, "he will do the same to you!" And that was how I ended. Then, another time, at Pentecost, I preached and asked the children, "Who comes at Pentecost?" And the children looked at each other and said, "The Holy Spirit!" And still not satisfied, I asked: "And who is the Holy Spirit?" And I asked a child at the back. And he replied, "The paralytic!" He couldn't say, "Paraclete"! We enjoyed ourselves. I laughed a lot. When I was parish priest, it was mostly with the children. And we haven't mentioned the children's party! At that party we burned the devil. It was a way of doing St Ignatius' Meditation on the Two Standards with the children. On the one hand there was the devil, on the other an angel. I made a big devil out of fabric and put bangers inside. There was a catechesis. Then I showed a film for the children, and instead the children went to play. Then there was lunch … and then we went

48

from the Collegio Massimo to the parish. We walked as if in procession. We were all very serious. The children knew, and shouted: "Let's burn the devil!" and then the fire was lit. Everyone was cheering. Off went the fireworks! The children were having a great time. It was theatre that helped them to learn. For me it was a way to make them do the third exercise of the worst week of the *Spiritual Exercises*. In that exercise St Ignatius wants to stimulate the capacity to condemn evil and produce hatred for sin.

'But it didn't stop there. All the children had a ticket with something they wanted to ask God for. They put those tickets in a little bag. And there was a great big angel made of polystyrene with lots of helium balloons. The angel wore a sign with the address of the parish church. We prayed. We said, "We have defeated the devil, and now we will pray to God who is our Father." And we released the angel, which, thanks to the balloons, rose up and up. And then everyone was praying … while the angel went up. The following Sunday we asked around to see if anyone had found the angel. Once, I remember, it had got as far as Uruguay, and they called from there! That was how I was as a parish priest. And then I took a lot of confessions. I was happy. I wanted to be a pastor, especially of children.'

Pope Francis and I remembered a book of answers to children's questions that we had once done together. 'When a child asks you a question, it's because he's worried. If you can create a certain interest and pick up the anxiety of the children, preaching is easy. And the important thing is to keep it short', he says to me.

REAL LOVE ISN'T RIGID

Even with adults, the simplicity of children makes me think of a directed rite such as those which attract big congregations in masses at local parishes, and which are experienced with great piety. I think of suggestions that lead priests to turn their backs on the faithful, to think about Vatican II, to use Latin. Not just for small groups but for everyone. I ask the Pope what he thinks about that.

The Pope replies: 'Pope Benedict did a just and magnanimous thing in accommodating a certain mentality on the part of some groups and people who were nostalgic and moving away. But that's an exception. That's why we talk about "extraordinary" rites. The ordinary rite of the Church isn't one of those. You need to approach it with magnanimity towards those who are used to a certain kind of prayer. But that isn't the ordinary rite. Vatican II and the *Sacrosanctum Concilium* need to be carried on as they are.[3] Talk of "reform of reform" is an error.'

'Apart from those who are sincere and ask for that possibility out of habit or devotion, can that desire express anything else? Are there dangers?' I ask.

The Pope replies: 'I wonder about that. For example, I'm always trying to understand what is behind people who are too young to have experienced the pre-Council liturgy and who want it anyway. Sometimes I have found myself confronted with very rigid people, an attitude of rigidity. And I've wondered: how come there's so much rigidity? Dig, dig, this rigidity always hides something: insecurity, sometimes even something else ... The rigidity is defensive. Real love isn't rigid.'

'And what about tradition? Some people mean it in a rigid sense', I insist.

'But no: tradition is flourishing!' he says. 'There's a traditionalism that's a rigid fundamentalism: it's not good. But fidelity implies growth. Tradition, in transmitting the deposit of faith from one era to another, grows and consolidates with the passing of time, as St Vincent of Lérins said in his *Commonitorium Primum*. I always read it from my breviary: *Ita etiam christianae religionis dogma sequatur has decet profectuum leges, ut annis scilicet consolidetur, dilatetur tempore, sublimetur aetate.*' ["The dogma of Christian religion must also follow these laws. It progresses, consolidating over the years, developing over time, deepening with age."]

'Father, you say that those who preach must recognize the heart of their community to seek where the desire for God is alive. But how do you recognize the heart of a Christian community?' I ask him.

He answers crisply: 'With contact, through being in the middle. The pastor is in the middle. You can't do that with books. I remember once an *Ad Audiendas* examination to qualify for taking confession. The candidate was a colleague of mine. They found him such a complicated and entirely abstract case that he replied to the examiner: "But this never happens in real life!" He was an ordinary person. The examiner's answer was: "Yes, but it does in books!" So, that's not how you recognize the heart of the community, the heart of people. You need to make contact. Or rather, you need to touch people, caress them. Touch is the most religious sense of the five. It's good to shake hands with children, with the sick: shake hands, caress ... Or in silence, look them in the eye. That too is contact. But it's the people that help you.'

I know, I know very well. All the people who see the Pope moving among the people know it: he never just walks straight on. Sometimes he even loses his balance. The contact, the caresses ...

'Sometimes', he goes on, thinking of the present day, 'I feel the desire to get out of the Popemobile. It often happens when I see little old ladies. I have a weakness for little old ladies, especially the sly ones. They speak to you with their eyes. The fact that people get enthusiastic when the Pope passes is beautiful. I couldn't do it. Perhaps I miss a bit of popular enthusiasm, of warmth. But they have it. And that's beautiful.'

'Some people say that, sometimes when you preach, you "berate". Others see that your words tends to probe, to stimulate, they lead listeners to examine their conscience in an atmosphere of consolation. What do you think about that?' I ask him. 'Yes, it's true', he replies straight away. 'Sometimes they berate. Sometimes you have to berate, sometimes stimulate sometimes both at the same time. Jesus did that too. Read the beatitudes of Luke: "Blessed, blessed, blessed … woe, woe, woe …"'

'GOD DOESN'T TAKE FRIGHT IN OUR WRETCHEDNESS'

Sitting on the sofa, Pope Francis assumes a thoughtful pose. Inspired by talking about people, he feels the need to explain something that I understand is important.

He says: 'There's a much-abused word: people talk a lot about populism, about populist politics, about populist programmes. But that's a mistake. People are not a logical category, it is not a mystical category, if we mean it in the sense that everything the people does is good or in the sense that the people is an angelic category. But no! It's a mythical category, if anything. I repeat: "mythical". A people is a historical and mythical category. A people is made through a process, with a commitment to a goal in mind or a common project. History is constructed out of this process of generations following on from one another within a people. You need a myth to understand the people. When you explain what a people is, you use logical categories because you have to explain it: they're necessary, certainly. But you don't explain the meaning of belonging to the people in that way. The world "people" has something more that can't be logically explained. Being part of the people means being part of a common identity made of social and cultural connections. And that isn't something automatic, it's a slow and difficult process ... towards a common project.'

'And the people of God?' I press.

'The people of God are capable of celebrating, of weeping. And this is not an idealization. But look at the people who followed Jesus! So many people followed him because they were enthusiasts. Jesus spoke with authority; he was a breath of fresh air. He wasn't like the doctors of the law who bowed the people down with many obligations. To preach to the people you have to look, you have to know how to look and how to listen, enter the living process, immerse yourself. But even the most stupid priest, or the most corrupt, is capable of that.'

I ask him for explanations, for an example. Who?

'I have a certain devotion to a corrupt priest. Eli, father of the priests Hophni and Phineas. He was old, he took a *laissez-faire* attitude, he was indolent. His priest sons exploited people.' The Pope is recalling the episode described in the First Book of Samuel. The protagonists here are Hannah – a woman distressed by her own barrenness, who tearfully begs God to give her a child – and the priest Eli, who watches her distractedly from a distance, sitting on a chair in the temple. Eli sees Hannah muttering but can't hear anything. So he thinks that the woman must be drunk and babbling.

'This is the courage of a woman of faith, tearfully asking the Lord for grace. Her prayer was a wager. She prayed as many mothers do. Eli, the priest, was a poor creature. I often feel very like him. How easily we judge people! Eli says to her: "Are you going to stay drunk for long?" And here again we see the humility of Hannah, who doesn't reply, "You're an old man, what do you know about it?" Instead, she says, "No, my Lord." And she says, "I am a grieving woman and I am not drunk: I am only bearing my heart to the Lord." Eli, in spite of his faults, had something inside, the spark of priestly fire. He listened to her and blessed her. That ability which the priesthood gives you to listen to people is something that you can lose through ideology, through the comfortable life, through attachment to power, to money, to many things. You can lose it. But you always have to ask that you are left with something that allows you to say the right thing and give your blessing. That old man gives me a feeling of tenderness. He was a sinner, but he was able to make a woman fertile with his blessing.'

It's a lovely story, and it expresses the Pope's heart. But this is how he goes on, with a related reflection.

'On the other hand,' he says, 'we ourselves remained closed. God's action in our lives is complex, it is mixed with our miseries. God acts, he is at work in us. I understand that what I say may be misunderstood, but once I heard that when World Youth Day was held in Rome, some people said: "Young people pray, they pray in that big field where the encounter with John Paul II was held … they enjoyed themselves in all sorts of ways." You see? Of course, of course, it's true. But be careful! You've got to take care. Sometimes people who say this kind of thing are scandalized because they don't know how to enter into human miseries! And that's what they are: miseries. It isn't about justifying everything, I'm not saying that, let's be clear. But you also have to understand that God isn't afraid of our miseries. So the priest mustn't feel discomfort, but he has to get his hands dirty with human miseries, he has to enter into human miseries in the awareness that the Lord is working in them. Someone who cannot enter into human miseries sees God on one side and on the other the absence of God, the void. But that's not how it is. You have to enter into human miseries. God is at work in them.'

'THE HOMILY IS ALWAYS POLITICAL'

'During the Te Deum you preached to the politicians. All the most important political authorities were assembled in Buenos Aires Cathedral. It is said that your homilies had a powerful impact. I know you like Dostoevsky: you told me that during our first interview in 2013. I read that on the occasion of the canonization of the River Plate martyrs, in the Auditorium del Salvador on 27 May 1988, you quoted *The Brothers Karamazov*: "He who doesn't believe in God won't believe in the people of God either." On 25 May 1999, in front of Carlos Menem and Fernando de la Rúa, you delivered a powerful and prophetic speech. Can a homily have a political impact?'

'Yes', he replies without hesitation, and with a firmness that didn't even wait for the end of my question. 'The homily is always political,' he goes on, 'because it is delivered in the *polis*, it is delivered in the midst of the people. Everything we do has a political dimension and is connected with the construction of civilization. We may say that even in the confessional, when you give absolution, you are constructing the common good. That is big politics. You need to have a big, wide politics. This isn't the ideological politics or the small politics of the economic crisis, however important that might be. Big politics is the one that, for the Christian, constructs the Kingdom of God. You can't say that Christians are apolitical. Christians must not be apolitical. You just have to read the Epistle to Diognetus to understand that. The citizen is called to involve himself, with a view to the common good, in a dialogue with all the active forces in society. We must find new forms of dialogue and coexistence in our pluralist societies. We must accept and respect differences, giving room to encounter and proximity. But how many Christians work shoulder to shoulder with many others for the common good: with brothers of other confessions and religious groups, social and political movements? We need new bonds, a new awareness of solidarity beyond any religious, ideological or political boundary. So the relationship between the Church and the public area needs to be thought and rethought, but preaching comes into this: it is not remote from the common good. In that sense the homily is always political.'

I go on, reminding him of the homily he delivered at the commemorative service for Néstor Kirchner, and he immediately says: 'Yes, he really didn't support me. Relations were very tense. When I found out that he had died, at three in the afternoon, two hours later I held a service of commemoration in the cathedral. The homily was improvised. I hadn't prepared the written text. I invited the people, and the church was full. There was no one there from the government. The atmosphere was tense: during Mass someone shouted at me. I said we were there to pray for him because the people, by electing him, had granted him the role of governing the country. The people had chosen him, and now they had to pray for him.'

'You also delivered ecumenical homilies and discourses, particularly with the Pentecostals. What spirit guided you?'

'In the stadium where these encounters took place there were charismatic Catholics and Protestants. There was a Catholic preacher and a Protestant one. Fr Cantalamessa went three times. I preached at the end, before the final blessing. But I knew lots of them very well. The director of the Curia in Buenos Aires was Protestant. First he was a bricklayer, but he had a fall. He recovered well, but he had to leave his former job and started working in the office. He was a really good man. Over time he became an administrator. He was an assistant to the pastor in his church. We often prayed together. Dialogue with the Pentecostal movement is important. One thing you have to be careful about is not to fall into a "theology of prosperity" that some people advocate. I am happy to engage in dialogue, and I trust some Pentecostal Protestant friends who know how things are and help me to talk to the right people.'

IF HE ISN'T CREATIVE, A PREACHER IS STERILE

Our conversation is reaching its conclusion. It's time for lunch. But I have one other topic that I'd like to talk to the Pope about: creativity.

'You sometimes use oppositions: "the confessional is neither a laundry nor a torture chamber", or "there is neither a saint without a past nor a sinner without a future". Why? Is it just an effective way of expressing yourself?'

'No, this has to do with opening up space for the Spirit so that it is free to move, rather than imposing ideas on it', he replies. 'Opposition opens up a path, a road to travel down. Speaking more generally, I must say that I love oppositions. Romano Guardini helped me with a book of his that is very important to me, *Der Gegensatz* ("Contrast"). He spoke of a polar opposition in which the two opposites do not cancel one another out. One pole doesn't even destroy the other. There is neither contradiction nor identity. For him, the opposition is resolved on a higher plane. But the bipolar tension remains in that solution. Tension remains; it is not cancelled out. Limits need to be overcome by not denying them. Oppositions help. Human life is structured in oppositional form. And that is what is now happening in the Church as well. Tensions do not necessarily need to be resolved and homogenized; they are not like contradictions.'

It seems to me that these polar oppositions some-times require a new language, one that isn't rigid and is hence creative.

'If it isn't creative, it's sterile', he answers dryly.

'So reading novels and poetry can help the preacher? In what way? It almost seems as if you have a poetic and popular language ... or rather poetic because it's popular', I suggest.

'Yes, it helps a lot', he says. 'Dostoevsky had helped me a lot with my preaching. For example, in *Karamazov*, when he writes about a child, barely eight years old, the son of a serving maid. He throws a stone and hits the paw of one of the master's dogs, so the master sets all the dogs on him. The child runs away and tries to escape the fury of the pack, but ends up being torn to pieces in front of the satisfied eyes of the master, a general, and the desperate eyes of the mother. And then in *Notes from Underground*, which is a gem. But poetry has helped me a lot as an inspiration too. Nino Costa is very dear to me. *Rassa nostrana*, dedicated to the Piedmontesi who work away from Italy and his father, who disappeared in Argentina, where he had emigrated to work. And then *La Consolà*. In that one, the bell-tower rings out over the countryside like a voice praying for all human misfortunes. And I've quoted Dante a few times. Certainly, his love for Mary: "Virgin mother, daughter of your son, humble and elevated beyond all creation." But also Paolo and

Francesca: "Love which forgives no love from the beloved ...." You see? Novels, literature can read the hearts of men, they help us to respond to desire, splendour and misery. It isn't theoretical. It helps you to preach, to know the heart.'

And he adds: 'I've quoted Fra Cristoforo from *I Promessi Sposi*. From Argentinian literature I've quoted *Don Segundo Sombra*, by Güiraldes. I like it when he says that, at first, life is like a fresh stream rushing down from above. Maturity is like a flowing river. And in the end life is like a serene and placid lake. But Hölderlin too!'

He quotes him in German, and I ask him to translate it. So he says: ' "Old age is calm and pious." And then there's the ode on his grandmother: "You've experienced so much." That's what I remember now.'

'Now it's my turn', the Pope says to me. And he is the one who moves the topic on to other subjects. I just have time to press 'stop' on the three tape-recorders that I've used because of my usual anxiety and the fear that one of them won't work. I've realized that this conversation has brought out the experience of a pastor with great simplicity and immediacy. But in his words there is a complex life full of 'polar oppositions', as he calls them. In the end he gets up and walks me to the lift. The door of the lift that takes me upstairs closes on his smile as he whispers: 'Let's always keep moving!'

4

NOT EVERYTHING IN LIFE IS BLACK AND WHITE: A PRIVATE MEETING WITH SOME POLISH JESUITS

During his apostolic trip to Poland on the occasion of the 31st World Youth Day (WYD), on 30 July 2016 – first vespers of St Ignatius of Loyola – at 5.00 p.m., Pope Francis met a group of 28 Polish Jesuits belonging to the two provinces of the Society of Jesus in the country and two lay collaborators, accompanied by the two Provincials, Fr Tomasz Ortmann and Fr Jakub Kołacz. The meeting was also attended by three other Jesuits: Fr Andrzej Majewski, Fr Federico Lombardi, then director of the Press Office of the Holy See, and Fr Antonio Spadaro, editor-in-chief of *La Civiltà Cattolica*.

The meeting took place at the archbishopric of Kraków in an atmosphere of great simplicity, spontaneity and warmth, and it was not without significant content for the life of the Order but also for the life of the Church more generally. Francis greeted everyone present one by one, lingering particularly with those he had known in the past. Then he sat down and began the dialogue, listening to the questions asked and replying in Italian. Fr Kołacz translated his words into Polish, even though the majority of those present understood Italian very well. Then the Pope received some presents. Before concluding the meeting, which lasted about 40 minutes in all, the Pope wanted to add an easily understandable recommendation connected to his recent Magisterium. With the approval of the Holy Father, we reproduce the dialogue here in all its immediacy, as it happened, also including personal memories. This should be understood as a witnessing that – as the reader will notice – brings together some impressions of the Pope's experience with the young people of the WYD, and also provides some significant pastoral lines.

'Your message gets to the heart of young people. How do you speak to them so effectively? Could you give us some advice about working with young people?'

'When I speak, I need to look people in the eyes. It isn't possible to look in the eyes of all of them, but I look into the eyes of this one, of that one, of this one … and everyone feels I am looking at them. It is something that comes to me spontaneously. This is how I do it with young people. But then young people, when you speak with them, ask questions. Today at lunch they asked some questions. They even asked me how I go to confession! They have no tact. They ask direct questions. And you always need to answer a young person with the truth. A young man asked me: "How do you confess?" And I started talking about myself. He said to me: "In my country there were scandals tied to priests, and we do not have the courage to go to confession with these priests who have lived these scandals. I can't do it." You see: they tell you the truth, at times they reprimand you … Young people speak directly. They want the truth or at least a clear "I don't know how to answer you". You never come across subterfuge with young people. The same with prayer. They asked me: "How do you pray?" If you answer with a theory, they remain disappointed. Young people are generous. But working with them also requires patience, a lot of patience. One of them asked me today: "What should I say to a friend who does not believe in God so that they can become a believer?" Here you see that at times young people need "recipes". So you must be ready to correct this attitude, which requires recipes and ready answers. I answered: "See that the last thing that you must do is to say something. Begin to do something. Then he or she will ask you explanations on how you live and why." Here you must be direct, direct with the truth.'

'What is the role of the Jesuit universities?'

'A university run by the Jesuits must be geared towards overall education, not one that is purely intellectual, but an education of the whole person. In fact, if the university becomes simply an academy of ideas or a "factory" of professionals, or a mentality centred on business prevails in its structure, then it is truly off the right road. We have the *Exercises* in hand. Here's the challenge: take the university along the path of the *Exercises*. This means risking the truth, and not the "closed truth" that no one discusses. The truth of the encounter with people is open and requires that we let ourselves make enquiries truly from reality. And the Jesuit university must be involved with the real life of the Church and the nation: this too is reality, a matter of fact. Particular attention must always be given to the marginalized, to the defence of those who need protection. And this – let us be clear – does not mean being a communist: it is simply being truly involved with reality. In this case, in particular a Jesuit university must be fully involved with reality expressing the social thought of the Church. The free-market thought that removes man and woman from the centre and puts money at the centre is not ours. The doctrine of the Church is clear, and it must move forward in this sense.'

'Why did you become a Jesuit?'

'When I entered the seminary, I already had a religious vocation. But at that time my confessor was anti-Jesuit. I also liked the Dominicans and their intellectual life. Then I fell ill and had to have an operation on my lung. Later another priest helped me spiritually.

I remember when I told my confessor that I had entered the Jesuits, he really didn't take it well. But here the irony of the Lord came into play. In fact, at that time they were conferring minor orders. The tonsure ceremony is performed in the first year of theological studies. The rector told me to go to Buenos Aires to the auxiliary bishop, Monsignor Oscar Villena, to get him to do the tonsure ceremony. I went to the House of Clergy, but they told me that Monsignor Villena was ill. In his place there was another monsignor, my former confessor, who was now a bishop! And he was the one who gave me my tonsure! And we have made our peace after many years … But, yes, I can say, my choice of the Society just happened by itself.'

'There are some recently ordained priests in this group. Do you have any advice for their future?'

'You know: the future comes from God. The most that we can do is what is possible in the future. And much of what is possible in the future is dominated by the evil spirit! A word of advice: the priesthood is truly a great grace: your priesthood as a Jesuit is soaked in the spirituality that you have experienced up to now: the spirituality of the *Suscipe* of St Ignatius.'[1]

At this point the encounter seemed to be drawing to a close, with the presentation to the Pontiff of gifts from some Jesuits who had accompanied a group of young people involved with Ignatian spirituality who had come to WYD from all over the world. Francis then wanted to add a piece of advice, and everyone sat down again.

'I would now like to add something. I ask you to work with seminarians. Above all, give them what you have received from the *Exercises*: the wisdom of discernment. The Church today needs to grow in its capacity for spiritual discernment. Some priestly education programmes run the risk of educating in the light of overly clear and distinct ideas, and therefore acting within parameters and criteria that are rigidly defined *a priori*, and that don't deal with concrete situations: "You must do this, you must not do this." And then the seminarians, when they become priests, find themselves in difficulty in accompanying the life of so many young people and adults. Because many of them ask: "Can you do this or can't you?" That's all. And many people leave the confessional disappointed. Not because the priest is bad, but because the priest doesn't have the ability to discern situations, to accompany them in authentic discernment. They don't have the necessary education. Today the Church needs to grow in discernment, in the ability to discern. And priests, above all, really need it for their ministry. That is why we need to teach it to seminarians and priests in their training: they are the ones usually entrusted with the confidences of the conscience of the faithful. Spiritual direction is not solely a priestly charism but also a lay one; it is true. But I repeat, you must teach this above all to priests, helping them in the light of the *Exercises* with the dynamic of pastoral discernment, which respects the law but knows how to go beyond it. This is an important task for the Society.

'I have often been struck by a thought of Fr Hugo Rahner.[2] He was a very clear thinker and writer. Fr Hugo said that the Jesuit must be a man with a nose for the supernatural, that is he must be a man gifted with a sense of the divine and the diabolical as they relate to events in human life and history. The Jesuit must therefore be capable of discerning both in the field of God and in the field of the devil. This is why in the *Exercises* St Ignatius asks to be introduced both to the intentions of the Lord of life and to those of the enemy of human nature and his lies. What he has written is bold, truly bold, but this is discernment! We need to train future priests not in general and abstract ideas, which are clear and distinct, but in this keen discernment of spirits, so that they can help people in their real life. We need truly to understand this: in life not everything is in black and white. No! In life shades of grey prevail. We must teach discernment in these grey areas.'

The encounter ended here, chiefly because of the need to continue with the day's schedule, as the Holy Father was reminded by his staff. Before taking his leave, however, Francis wanted once more to greet the Jesuits one by one, concluding with a final blessing.

5

DISTANCE MAKES US ILL: AN INTERVIEW WITH ULF JONSSON

During a meeting of the directors of the European cultural journals of the Society of Jesus, in mid-June 2016, I told Antonio Spadaro, director of *La Civiltà Cattolica*, of a desire that I had had in my heart for some time: to interview Pope Francis on the eve of his apostolic trip to Sweden, on 31 October 2016, to participate in the ecumenical celebration of the 500th anniversary of the Lutheran Reformation. I thought an interview was the best way to prepare the country for the message that the Pope planned to give to people during his visit. As director of the cultural journal of the Swedish Jesuits, *Signum*, I thought that this goal coincided neatly with our mission.

Ecumenism – like dialogue between the religions and with non-believers – is a subject close to the Pope's heart. He has expressed this in many ways. But above all, he himself is a man of reconciliation. Francis is deeply convinced that men and women must overcome barriers and fences of all kinds. He believes in what he calls 'the culture of encounter', so that all may co-operate in the common good of humanity. I wanted this vision of Francis to touch minds and hearts before the Pope's arrival in Sweden: the interview would be the best means to achieve such a goal. I said this to Fr Spadaro, with whom I pursued this idea until August, when together we reached the conclusion that it would be a good idea to present the Pope with this suggestion in such a way that he could decide whether to fulfil it or not. The Pope took the time to reflect on this opportunity. In the end his reply was positive: he gave us an appointment at the Casa Santa Marta, on Saturday, 24 September, in the late afternoon.

It was a really beautiful day, warm and sunny. Driving through the Roman traffic with Fr Spadaro, I felt anxious but content. We arrived 15 minutes early. We expected to have to wait, but instead we were immediately invited up to the floor where the Pope has his room. When the lift opened, I saw a Swiss Guard, who greeted us courteously. I could hear the Pope speaking cordially with other people in Spanish, but I couldn't see him. After a while he appeared with two people, conversing amiably. He greeted me and Fr Spadaro with a smile, ushering us into his room: he would be there in a moment.

I was impressed by the simplicity and the warm familiarity of his welcome. We had been told in the porters' lodge that the Pope had had a busy day, and that he might be tired as a result, so I was very struck to see him so energetic and relaxed.

The Pope came into his room and invited us to sit wherever we liked. I sat down on an armchair, and Fr Spadaro sat down opposite me. The Pope sat down on the sofa between the two armchairs. I wanted to introduce myself in Italian, which is limited but enough to understand and converse simply. After exchanging some pleasantries with the Pope, we turned on the tape-recorders and began the conversation. Fr Sparado had translated some questions from English that I wanted to ask the Pope, and for which I had done some preparation, but then the conversation between us flowed naturally, in a friendly atmosphere without any artificiality. Above all, it was forthright and direct, with no waffle and with none of that atmosphere that one expects of meetings with great leaders or important dignitaries. I no longer have any doubt that Pope Francis loves conversation, communicating with other people. Sometimes he takes time to reflect before answering, and his replies always convey a sense of serious involvement, but are not ponderous or sad. In fact, during our visit he demonstrated his sense of humour several times.

————

'Holy Father, on 31 October you will visit Lund and Malmö to participate in the ecumenical

Commemoration of the 500 Years of the Reformation, organized by the Lutheran World Federation and the Pontifical Council for the Promotion of Christian Unity. What are your hopes and expectations for this historical event?'

'In a word: to come close. My hope and expectation are to get closer to my brothers and sisters. Closeness is good for all of us. Distance, on the other hand, makes us ill. When we become distant from one another, we close ourselves up inside ourselves and become individual entities, incapable of meeting one another. We are held back by fear. We have to learn to transcend ourselves in order to meet others. If we don't, then we Christians also fall ill with division. My expectation to take a step closer, to get closer to my brothers and sisters who live in Sweden.'

'In Argentina the Lutherans are rather a small community. Have you managed to have any direct contact with them in the past?'

'Yes, some. I remember the first time I set foot inside a Lutheran church: it was in their main church in Argentina, on Calle Esmeralda in Buenos Aires. I was 17. I remember that day very clearly. A colleague of mine, Axel Bachmann, was getting married. He was the uncle of the Lutheran theologian Mercedes García Bachmann. And Mercedes's mother, Ingrid, worked in the same laboratory as me. That was the first time I had witnessed a Lutheran celebration. The second time

was a more powerful experience. We Jesuits have the
Theology Faculty in San Miguel, where I taught. Near
by, less than ten kilometres away, was the Lutheran
Theology Faculty. The rector was a Hungarian, Béla
Leskó, who was a very good man. I had very cordial
relations with him. I was a professor and had the chair
of Spiritual Theology. I invited the professor of Spiritual
Theology from that faculty, a Swede, Anders Ruuth, to
give lessons in spirituality with me. I remember that
that was a truly difficult moment for my soul. I placed
a great deal of trust in him, and opened my heart to
him. He helped me a lot at that time. Then he was sent
to Brazil – he knew Portuguese as well – and then he
came back to Sweden. There he published his disser-
tation on "The Universal Church of the Kingdom of
God", which was published in Brazil in the late 1970s.
It was a critical text. He wrote it in Swedish, but there
was a chapter in English. He sent it to me and I read
that chapter in English: it was a gem. Then time passed
… In the meantime I became an auxiliary bishop in
Buenos Aires. One day I had a visit from the then archbishop primate of Uppsala at the bishop's residence.
Cardinal Quarracino wasn't there. He invited me to
their Mass in Calle Azopardo, in the Iglesia Nórdica of
Buenos Aires, formerly the "Swedish Church". I talked
to him about Anders Ruuth, who had come back to
Argentina to celebrate a wedding. On that occasion
we saw each other again, but it was the last time: one

of his two sons, the musician – the other one was a doctor – called me one day to tell me he was dead.

'Another chapter in my relations with the Lutherans concerns the Church of Denmark. I had a good relationship with the pastor at the time, Albert Andersen, who is now in the United States. He invited me twice to deliver a sermon. The first was in a liturgical context. On that occasion it was very delicate: to avoid causing embarrassment about participation in Communion, on that day he celebrated not Mass but a baptism. He went on to invite me to give a lecture to their young people. I remember having a very heated long-distance discussion with him when he was back in the United States. The pastor chided me a great deal because of what I had said about a law concerning religious problems in Argentina. But I must say that he chided me honestly and sincerely, like a real friend. When he returned to Buenos Aires, I went and apologized to him, because basically the way I had expressed myself in that case had been a bit aggressive. Then I was also very close to Pastor David Calvo, another Argentinian, of the Iglesia Evangélica Luterana Unida. He too was a good person.

'I also remember that on the "Day of the Bible", which was celebrated in Buenos Aires at the end of September, I went back to the first church that I had visited as a young man, in Calle Esmeralda. And there I met Mercedes García Bachmann. We had a conversation. That was the last institutional encounter that I had with Lutherans when I was archbishop of Buenos Aires. But I went on to have relationships with individual Lutheran friends on a personal level. But the man who did so much good in my life was Anders Ruuth: I think of him with much affection and gratitude. When the primate archbishop of the Church of Sweden came here to see me, we referred to that friendship between the two of us. I remember clearly when Archbishop Antje Jackelén came here to the Vatican in May 2015 on an official visit: she gave a very nice speech. I also met her again on the occasion of the canonization of Maria Elisabeth Hesselblad.[1] Then I was able to meet her husband as well: they are truly lovely people. Then, as Pope, I went and preached at the Lutheran church in Rome. I was very struck by the questions I was asked then: the question from the child, and a question a woman asked about inter-communion. Profound and beautiful questions. And the pastor of that church is very good!'

'In ecumenical dialogue, the different communities should try to enrich themselves mutually with the best of their traditions. What could the Catholic Church learn from the Lutheran tradition?'

'Two words come to my mind: "reform" and "Scripture". Let me try to explain. The first is the word "reform". At first Luther's reform was a gesture of reform during a difficult time for the Church. Luther wanted to find a remedy for a complex situation. And then that gesture – not least because of political situations, let us also think of *cuius regio, eius religio*[2] – became a "state" of separation, and not a "process" of reform of the whole Church, which is in fact fundamental because the Church is *semper reformanda*. The second word is "Scripture", the Word of God. Luther took a great step by putting the Word of God into the hands of the people. Reform and Scripture are the two fundamental things that we can deepen by looking at the Lutheran tradition. The General Congregations of Cardinals before the conclave come to mind, and how the request for reform was vividly present in our discussions.'

'Only once before has a Pope visited Sweden, and that was when John Paul II came in 1989. It was a time of ecumenical enthusiasm, and of a deep desire for unity between Catholics and Lutherans. Since then the ecumenical movement seems to have lost its impetus, and new obstacles have emerged. How should we deal with these? What, in your view, are the best ways of promoting Christian unity?'

'Clearly it is up to theologians to continue to engage in dialogue and study the issues: on this there is no doubt. Theological dialogue must continue, because it is a path to follow. I think of the results that have been achieved along this path with the great ecumenical document on justification; that was a great step forward.[3] Certainly, after that step I imagine that it will not be easy to go forward because of the different ways of understanding some theological questions. I asked Patriarch Bartholomew if the story about Patriarch Athenagoras was true, that he had said to Paul VI: "Let the two of us go ahead, and we will put the theologians on an island to discuss among themselves." He told me that this remark was true. But, yes, theological dialogue must continue, even though it won't be easy.

'Personally I also believe that enthusiasm must shift towards common prayer and works of mercy, working together to help the sick, the poor, the imprisoned. Doing something together is a deep and effective form of dialogue. I'm also thinking about education. It is important to work together, and not in a sectarian way. There is one criterion that should be very clear in every case: proselytism is a sin in the ecclesiastical field. Benedict XVI said that the Church grows not through proselytism but through attraction. Proselytism is a sinful attitude. It would be like transforming the Church into an organization. Speaking, praying, working together: that is the path that we must take. You see, in unity the one who never makes a mistake is the enemy, the devil. When Christians are persecuted and killed, it is because they are Christians and not because they are Lutherans, Calvinists, Anglicans, Catholics or Orthodox. There is an ecumenism of blood.

'I remember an episode that I experienced with the parish priest from the parish of St Joseph at Wandsbek in Hamburg. He brought forward the cause of the martyrs guillotined by Hitler for teaching the catechism. They were guillotined one after the other. After the first two, who were Catholic, a Lutheran pastor was sentenced for the same reason. The blood of the three was mixed. The parish priest told me that it was impossible for him to continue with the cause of beatification of the two Catholics without including the Lutheran: their blood had mixed! But I also remember the homily given by Paul VI in Uganda in 1964, which mentioned the Catholic and Lutheran martyrs together, united. That is also happening in our own time: the Orthodox, the Coptic martyrs being killed in Libya … It's an ecumenism of the blood. So: praying together, working together and understanding the ecumenism of the blood.'

'One of the major causes of anxiety in our time is the spread of terrorism dressed up in religious terms. The meeting in Assisi put the emphasis on inter-religious dialogue.[4] How did you experience it?'

'All the religions that had had contact with Sant'Egidio were there. I met the people that Sant'Egidio had contacted: I didn't choose who to meet. But there were very many of them, and the encounter was very respectful and without syncretism. We all talked together about peace and we asked for peace. Together we spoke out loudly for peace, for what the religions really want. You can't make war in the name of religion, of God: that is blasphemy, it is satanic. Today I received about 400 people who were in Nice during the terrorist attack there and I greeted the victims, the wounded, people who lost wives or husbands or children. The madman who committed that massacre believed he was doing it in God's name. The poor man, he was deranged! Charitably we can say that he was a deranged man who tried to use the name of God to justify his actions. That's why the meeting at Assisi is very important.'

'But recently you also spoke about another form of terrorism: the terrorism of gossip. In what sense, and how do you defeat it?'

'Yes, there is an internal and underground terrorism which is a vice that it is hard to eradicate. I describe the vice of murmurings and gossip as a form of terrorism: it is a form of deep violence that we all have at our disposal in our souls, and which requires profound conversion. The problem with this terrorism is that all of us are capable of it. Every one of us is capable of becoming a terrorist just by our use of language. I'm not talking about the arguments that we have openly, like wars. I'm talking about a sneaky, hidden kind of terrorism that is done by throwing out words like bombs, and which does a great deal of harm. The root of this terrorism lies in Original Sin, and is a form of criminality. It is a way of gaining space for oneself by destroying the other. So what is necessary is a deep conversion of the heart to defeat that temptation, and we need to examine ourselves a lot on that point. The sword kills many people, but language kills more, the Apostle James says in the third volume of his Epistle. The tongue is a small part of the body, but it can develop a fire of evil and consume the whole of our lives. The tongue can fill with deadly poison. That terrorism is difficult to quell.'

'Religion can be a blessing, but also a curse. The media often report news stories about conflicts between religious groups across the world. Some claim that the world would be more peaceful if religion didn't exist. What do you say in response to such criticism?'

'It is the idolatries that are at the base of a religion, not the religion itself! There are idolatries connected to religion: the idolatry of money, of enmities, of space greater than time, the greed of the territoriality of space. There is an idolatry of the conquest of space, of dominion, which attacks religions like a malignant virus. And idolatry is a false religion, a wrong religiosity. I call it an "immanent transcendence" – in other words, a contradiction. In fact, true religions are the development of humanity's capacity to transcend itself towards the absolute. The religious phenomenon is transcendent, and it has to do with truth, beauty, goodness and unity. If this openness does not exist, there is no transcendence, there is no true religion: there is idolatry. Openness to transcendence absolutely cannot be the cause of terrorism, because that openness is always united with the quest for truth, beauty, goodness and unity.'

'You have often spoken in very clear terms about the terrible situation of Christians in some parts of the Middle East. Is there still hope of a more peaceful and humane development for Christians in that area?'

'I hope the Lord will not leave his people on their own. He will not abandon them. When we read of the hard trials of the people of Israel in the Bible, or when we remember the trials of the martyrs, we see how the Lord always comes to the aid of his people. We remember in the Old Testament the killing of the seven children with their mother in the Book of Maccabees. Or the martyrdom of Eleazar. Certainly martyrdom is one of the forms of Christian life. We recall St Polycarp and the Letter to the Church of Smyrna, which gives us the story of the circumstances of his arrest and death. Yes, at the moment the Middle East is a land of martyrs. Without a doubt we can speak about martyrs and martyred Syria. I would like to quote a personal memory that has stayed in my heart: in Lesbos I met a father with two children. He told me he was very much in love with his wife. He was a Muslim, and she was a Christian. When the terrorists came, they wanted her to take off her cross, but she wouldn't let them, and they cut her throat in front of her husband and children. And he went on: "I love her so much, I love her so much." Yes, she is a martyr. But the Christian knows there is hope. The blood of the martyrs is the seed of Christianity: we have known that for ever.'

'You are the first non-European pope for over 1,200 years, and have often highlighted the life of the Church in the regions of the world that are considered "peripheral". Where, in your view, will the Catholic Church have its liveliest communities in the next 20 years? And in what way will the churches of Europe be able to contribute to the Catholicism of the future?'

'This is a question to do with space, with geography. I am allergic to talking about spaces, but I always say that you can see things better from the periphery than from the centre. The liveliness of ecclesiastical communities depends not on space, on geography, but on the spirit. It is true that the young churches have a fresher spirit, and on the other hand there are aged churches, churches that are slightly sleepy, that seem interested only in preserving their space. In those cases I don't say that they lack spirit: it's there, yes, but it is enclosed in a structure, in a rigid way, fearful of losing space. In the churches in some countries you can actually see that they lack freshness. In this sense freshness from the peripheries gives more room to the spirit. You have to avoid the effects of churches ageing badly. It does us good to read the third chapter of Joel, where he says that the old will dream dreams and the young will have visions. In the dreams of the old lies the possibility that our young people will have new visions, that they will have a future again. Instead, the churches are sometimes closed in terms of their programmes, their programming. I admit it: I know they're necessary, but I have a great deal of trouble placing much hope in organizational structures. The spirit is ready to push us, to go forward. And the spirit is found in the ability to dream and the capacity for prophecy. For me that is a challenge for the whole Church, the challenge to its capacity for freshness. That is why in Kraków, during World Youth Day,[5] I recommended that young people talk to their grandparents. The young Church rejuvenates more when young people talk to old people, and when the old people are able to have big dreams, because that makes the young people prophesy. If the young don't prophesy, the Church lacks air.'

'Your visit to Sweden will touch one of the most secularized countries in the world. A large part of its population doesn't believe in God, and religion plays quite a modest part in public life and society. In your view, what does a person lose by not believing in God?'

'It isn't a matter of losing something. It's about not adequately developing a capacity for transcendence. The path of transcendence gives space to God, and for that small steps are important too, even the one from being an atheist to being an agnostic. For me the problem is when one is closed and considers one's life as perfect in itself, and hence closed up and with no need for radical transcendence. But to open up others to transcendence one does not need to use a lot of words and discourse. Those who live transcendence are visible: they are a living witness. During the lunch I had at Kraków with some young people, one of them asked me: "What should I say to a friend of mine who doesn't believe in God? How can I convert him?" I said: "The last thing you must do is to say anything. Act! Live! Then, seeing your life, your witness, the other person will ask you why you live like that." I am convinced that those who do not believe or do not seek God may not have experienced the restlessness that comes from bearing witness. And that is very much tied to affluence. Restlessness is difficult to find in affluence. That is why I think that against atheism, and hence closure to transcendence, the only things that really work are prayer and witness.'

'Catholics in Sweden are a small minority, mostly composed of immigrants from various nations in the world. You will meet some of them when you celebrate Mass in Malmö on 1 November. How do you see the role of Catholics in a culture like that of Sweden.'

'I see a healthy coexistence in which each one can live their own faith and express their own witness by living an open and ecumenical spirit. You can't be

Catholic and sectarian. You have to strive to be with others. "Catholic" and "sectarian" are contradictions in terms. That's why at first I wasn't planning to celebrate Mass for the Catholics on this trip: I wanted to insist on ecumenical witnessing. Then I thought hard about my role as pastor of a flock of Catholics who will also come from other nearby countries, such as Norway and Denmark. Then, responding to the fervent requests of the Catholic community, I decided to celebrate a Mass, extending the trip by a day. In fact, I wanted Mass to be celebrated not on the same day and not in the same place as the ecumenical meeting, to avoid confusing plans. The deep significance of the ecumenical encounter needs to be preserved in its profound significance according to a spirit of unity, which is my desire. This has created organizational problems, I know, because I will be in Sweden on All Saints Day, which is important here in Rome. But to avoid misunderstanding, that was how I wanted it to be.'

'You are a Jesuit. Since 1897 the Jesuits have carried out their activities in Sweden with parishes, spiritual exercises, the journal *Signum* and, over the last 15 years, thanks to the Newman Institute. What commitments and what values should characterize the apostolate of the Jesuits in this country today?'

'I believe that the first task of the Jesuits in Sweden is that of favouring in every way dialogue with those who live in a secularized society and with non-believers: talking, sharing, understanding, standing alongside. So clearly you need to favour ecumenical dialogue. The model, for Swedish Jesuits, must be St Peter Faber, who was always travelling, and who was guided by a good, open spirit. The Jesuits don't have a quiet structure. We must have restless hearts and structures, yes, restless ones.'

'Who is Jesus for Jorge Mario Bergoglio?'

'Jesus, for me, is He who has looked at me with mercy and has saved me. My relationship with Him has always had that basis and foundation. Jesus has given meaning to my life here on earth and hope for the future life. He looked at me with mercy, He took me, He set me on my path ... And He gave me an important grace: the grace of shame. The whole of my spiritual life is written in Chapter 16 of Ezekiel. Especially in the last verses, when the Lord reveals that He will establish his covenant with Israel, saying to them: "You will know that I am the Lord, so that you remember and are ashamed and, in your confusion, you will never again open your mouth when I have pardoned you for what you have done." Shame is positive: it makes you act, but it makes you understand your place, who you are, preventing any pride and vanity.'

'One last word, Holy Father, about this trip to Sweden ...'

'What comes spontaneously for me to add now is simple: go, walk together! Do not stay closed in rigid perspectives, because in them there is no possibility of reform.'

The Pope, Fr Spadaro and I spent about an hour and a half in conversation. At the end Francis walked us to the lift. He asked us to pray for him. The doors closed as he waved to us with a radiant smile that I will never forget.

It was already dark outside. The illuminated dome of St Peter's revealed its splendour as we climbed into the car to be back in time for dinner in the community of *La Civiltà Cattolica*.

6

Have Courage and Prophetic Daring: A dialogue with the Jesuits of the General Congregation

On 24 October 2016 Pope Francis met the Jesuits gathered in their 36th General Congregation. He arrived in an economy car a few minutes before nine o'clock. After greeting the Father General and the others who were waiting for him, he went to the Aula of the Congregation, where he joined all the delegates in prayer. Then he gave a speech. After a break, he entered into a frank and cordial dialogue with the delegates, who spontaneously asked him some questions. The Pope did not want them to be selected in advance, and did not want to know them beforehand. This produced an extremely intimate encounter that lasted for about an hour and a half. In the end Francis greeted those present individually. We reproduce the questions and answers below. In the Aula, for practical reasons, the questions were asked in groups of three. The following text reproduces the Pope's answers in their entirety and, for ease of reading, separates the questions, quoting their basic thrust. The text preserves the tone and meaning of the oral conversation.

'Holy Father, you are a living example of prophetic daring. How do you communicate that audacity so effectively? How can we do it too?'

'Courage is not just about speaking out but about knowing how to do it well, when and how to do it. First of all one must discern whether one should speak out or not. Courage is constitutive of all apostolic action. And today, more than ever, we need courage and prophetic audacity. We need a *parresia* for today, the prophetic audacity of having no fear.[1] It is noteworthy that this was the first thing that John Paul II said when he was elected Pope: "Do not be afraid." He knew all the problems of the Eastern countries, and audacity led him to confront them all.

'What is the prophetic audacity that is asked of us today? We must discern this. That is, where should this prophetic audacity be channelled? It is an attitude born of the *magis*.[2] And the *magis* is *parresia*. The *magis* is founded on God, who is always greater. Looking at that ever greater God, discernment deepens and seeks the places to channel the audacity. I believe that this is your work in this Congregation: to discern where the *magis*, the prophetic audacity, the *parresia*, must be directed.

'Sometimes, prophetic audacity joins with diplomacy, with a work of persuasion accompanied by powerful signs. For example, in some countries prophetic audacity is called upon to combat widespread corruption. Corruption, to give an example, such as when the constitutional period of a term of office ends and someone seeks to reform the constitution in order to remain in power. I believe that here the Society, in its work of teaching and raising social awareness, must work with audacity to convince everyone that a country cannot grow if it does not respect the legal principles that that country itself has put in place to ensure their own future governability.'

'Father, the way in which colonizers have treated indigenous peoples has been a serious problem. The appropriation of the land by the colonizers was a grave event whose repercussions are still felt today. What do you think about this?'

'First of all, it must be said that today we are more aware of the significance of the richness of the indigenous peoples, especially when, both politically and culturally, other forces tend to suppress them even more through globalization conceived as a "sphere", a globalization where everything becomes standardized. Today, our prophetic audacity, our consciousness, must be on the side of inculturation. And our image of globalization should be not the sphere but the polyhedron. I like the geometric figure of the polyhedron, because it is one but has different faces. It expresses how unity is created while preserving the identities of peoples, of people, of cultures. That is the richness that today we have to give to the process of globalization, because otherwise it is homogenizing and destructive.

'The process of a standardizing and destructive globalization involves the annihilation of indigenous cultures, which in fact need to be recovered. And we must recover them with the correct hermeneutic, which facilitates this task for us. This hermeneutic is not the same as it was at the time of colonization. The hermeneutic of that time was to seek the conversion of the peoples, to broaden the Church ... thus abolishing indigenous independence. It was a centralist type of hermeneutic, where the dominant empire somehow imposed its faith and culture. It is understandable that people thought that way at the time, but today a radically different hermeneutic is necessary. We must interpret things differently, valuing all peoples, their cultures, their languages. We must help this process of inculturation, which has become increasingly important since Vatican II.

'However, I want to refer to attempts at inculturation present in the early days of the missions. These initiatives were born of an experience like that of Paul with the Gentiles. The Holy Spirit showed him very clearly that the Gospel was to be inculturated in the Gentile peoples. The same thing was repeated in the era of missionary expansion. Consider, for example, the experience of Matteo Ricci and Roberto de Nobili.[3] They were pioneers, but a hegemonic conception of Roman centralism put a halt to that experience, interrupted it. It prevented a dialogue in which cultures were respected. And this happened because they interpreted social customs with a religious hermeneutic. Respect for the dead, for example, was confused with idolatry. Hermeneutics play a central role here. At this moment I believe that it is important, with this greater awareness that we now have regarding indigenous peoples, to support the expression, the culture, of each one of them ... and, in the same way, evangelization, which also touches the liturgy and reaches the expressions of worship. And the Congregation for Divine Worship accepts this.

'I'll end with a memory that touches on moral theology. When I was a student of theology, I was given a job as a librarian. When reviewing a Mexican text on morality from the 1700s, written in a question-and-answer format, I found a question that read: "Is sexual union between a Spaniard and an indigenous woman a mortal sin?" The answer of the moralist, who was a Dominican, made me laugh: "The matter is serious, therefore it is a serious sin according to the matter, but since the consequence of this would be one more Christian to enlarge the kingdom of God, it is not as serious as if it happened in Europe."'

'In your speech you clearly proposed a morality that is based on discernment. How do you suggest that we proceed in the field of morality with regard to this dynamic of discernment of moral situations? It seems to me that it is not possible to stay with an interpretation of a subsumed application of the norm that is limited to seeing particular situations as cases of the general norm.'

'Discernment is the key element: the capacity for discernment. I note the absence of discernment in the formation of priests. We run the risk of becoming accustomed to "black or white", to that which is legal. We are rather closed, in general, to discernment. One thing is clear: today, in a number of seminaries, a rigidity has been introduced which is a long way from a discernment of situations. And that is dangerous, because it can lead us to a conception of morality that has a casuistic intention. It appears in different formulations, but it is always along the same lines. This makes me very worried. This is what I said in a meeting with the Jesuits in Kraków during the World Youth Day. The Jesuits asked me what I thought the Society could do, and I replied that one important task of the Society is to train seminarians and priests in discernment.

'I and those of my generation, perhaps not the youngest here, but my generation and some of the later ones too, were educated in a decadent scholasticism.

We studied theology and philosophy from manuals. It was a decadent scholasticism. For example, to explain the "metaphysical continuum" – it makes me laugh every time I think of it – we were taught the theory of the "*puncta inflata*".[4] When the great scholasticism began to lose strength, it was replaced by that decadent scholasticism which at least my generation and others have studied.

'It was that decadent scholasticism that provoked the casuistical attitude. It is curious: the course on the "sacrament of penance" in the faculty of theology, in general – not everywhere – was presented by teachers of sacramental morality. The whole moral sphere was restricted to "you can", "you cannot", "so far but no further". In an *Ad Audiendas* examination a companion of mine, when asked a very intricate question, said very simply: "But Father, please, these things do not happen in reality!" And the examiner replied, "But they're in the books!"

'It was a morality very foreign to discernment. At that time there was the *cuco*,[5] the spectre of situational morality ... I think Bernard Häring was the first to start looking for a new way to help moral theology to flourish again.[6] Obviously, in our day moral theology has made much progress in its reflections and in its maturity; it is no longer "casuistry".

'In the field of morality we must advance without lapsing into situationalism: rather, it is necessary to bring forward again the great wealth contained in the dimension of discernment; this is characteristic of the great scholasticism. There is something we should note: St Thomas and St Bonaventure affirm that the general principle holds for all, but – they say it explicitly – as one moves to the particular, the question becomes diversified, and many nuances arise without altering the principle. This scholastic method has its validity. It is the moral method used by the Catechism of the Catholic Church. And it is the method that was used in the last apostolic exhortation, *Amoris laetitia*, after the discernment made by the whole Church through the two Synods. The morality applied in *Amoris laetitia* is Thomistic, but that of the great St Thomas himself, not of the author of the "*puncta inflata*".

'It is evident that, in the field of morality, one must proceed with scientific rigour, and with love for the Church and discernment. There are certain points of morality on which only in prayer can one have sufficient light to continue reflecting theologically. And on this, allow me to repeat it, one must do "theology on one's knees". Theology cannot be done without prayer. This is a key point and it must be done this way.'

'There are many legends about the Society: positive ones, from those who like us, and stories that are rather darker, from those who do not. To you, who love us and know us well, I want to ask: what things would you like us to pay attention to?'

'I find it a little difficult to respond, because we need to see where the criticisms are coming from. It is difficult because, in my situation and in the environment in which I move, criticisms of the Society tend to have a predominantly restorationist flavour. In other words, they are criticisms that dream of the restoration of a Society that might once have been attractive, because that was its time, but which is no longer desirable in our day, because it is no longer God's time for the Society. I think this is the kind of argument behind the criticism. But on this point the Society must be faithful to what the Spirit tells it.

'Critiques also depend on who it is that is making them. We should discern where they come from. I think that sometimes even the most malicious critic can say something that helps me. I think we must listen to all the critiques and discern them, and not close the door to any criticism, because we risk getting used to closing doors. And that's not good. After discernment one may say: this criticism has no foundation, and I can set it aside. But we must submit to discernment all of the criticism that we hear, I would say daily, personally, but always with good will, with openness of heart and before the Lord.'

'We live in a world characterized by political and religious polarizations. You, in fact, have lived different experiences in your life, as provincial and as archbishop of Buenos Aires. From your experience, what suggestions for us can you make of ways to confront these situations of polarization, especially when our brothers are involved in them?'

'I think that politics in general, big politics, has been increasingly degraded into small politics. Not only in partisan politics in each country, but also in sectoral politics within the same continent. I wanted to address this specific question – because I was asked to – with the three speeches about Europe: the two in Strasbourg and the one delivered at the Charlemagne Prize. The French bishops have just issued a communiqué on politics which picks up or follows on from one delivered 15 or 20 years ago, *"Réhabiliter la politique"*, which was very important. That declaration was timely: it gave force to politics, to politics as craftsmanship used to build the unity of peoples and the unity of a people with all the diversity that is within them. In general, the opinion I hear is that politicians are on the wane. Countries lack those great politicians who were able to devote themselves seriously to their ideals and were not afraid of dialogue or struggle, but went ahead, with intelligence and with the charism specific to politics. Politics is one of the highest forms of charity. Great politics. And here I think that polarization doesn't help. On the contrary, what helps in politics is dialogue.'

'What is your experience of the brothers in the Society, in terms of their role, and how can those with the vocation to be a brother be attracted to the Society?'

'My experience with the brothers has always been very positive. The brothers I lived with during my time as a student were wise men, very wise. They had a wisdom different from that of scholastics or the priests. Today, even brothers who have studied a great deal and who have leadership positions in the Institutes still have a certain quality that is different from the priests. And I think this has to be preserved – the wisdom, that special quality of wisdom that comes from being a brother.

'What's more, in the brothers I knew, I was impressed by their special sense, the ability to "smell", that they had when they said, for example: "Watch that father, I think he needs special help." ... The brothers I have known often had great discretion. And they helped! The brother realized, before any other community members, what was happening. I don't know how to put it. I believe that there is a specific grace here, and we must find what God's will is for the brother right now, and we also need to try to find how to express it.'

'I would like to hear you say when the prophecy of Isaiah will be fulfilled: "They will beat their swords into ploughshares ..." In my continent, Africa, we already have sufficient means to kill us all ten times over.'

'Working for peace is urgent. I said, more than a year and a half ago, that we are in World War III, in bits and pieces. Now the bits are coming together more and more. We are at war. We must not be naïve. The world is at war, and several countries are paying the price. Let us think of the Middle East, of Africa: they are in a state of constant war. Wars that derive from a whole history of colonization and exploitation. It is true that countries have their independence, but often the country that gave them independence has reserved the subsoil for itself. Africa remains a target of exploitation for the riches it has, even by countries that did not even think about this continent in the past. Africa is always viewed from the perspective of exploitation. And clearly this provokes wars.

'Furthermore, in some countries there is the problem of ideologization, which leads to major fractures. I believe that at this juncture working for peace, besides being one of the beatitudes, is a priority. When will peace come? I do not know if it will come before the Son of Man, but I do know, on the other hand, that we need to work for peace as much as possible, through politics, through coexistence. It can come. It can. With the Christian attitudes that the Lord shows us in the Gospel, much can be done, much is being done, and we move forward. Sometimes this comes at a high price, for ourselves. And still we carry on. Martyrdom is part of our vocation.'

'Can we be saved alone? What is the relationship between community salvation and personal salvation?'

'No one is saved alone. I believe that this principle must remain very clear: salvation is for the People of God. No one is saved alone. The one who wishes to save himself, to go along his own path to fulfilment, will end with that adjective that Jesus uses so many times: hypocritical. He ends in hypocrisy. To be saved alone, to attempt to save oneself, with an elitist attitude, is hypocrisy. The Lord has come to save everyone.'

'Is it good to study theology in a context of real life?'

'My advice is that everything that young people study and experience in their contact with different contexts should also be subject to personal and community discernment and taken to prayer. There must be academic study, contact with real life not only at the periphery but at the boundary of the periphery, prayer and personal and community discernment. If a community of students does all this, I am at peace. When one of those things is missing, I start to worry. If study is lacking, then one can talk nonsense or idealize situations in a simplistic way. If there is no real and objective context, accompanied by those who know the environment and help, foolish idealisms can arise. If there is a lack of prayer and discernment, we can be very good sociologists or political scientists, but we will not have the evangelical audacity and the evangelical cross that we must bear, as I said at the beginning.'

'The Society, after the 35th General Congregation, has gone some way toward the understanding of

environmental challenges. We received *Laudato si'*
with joy. We feel that the Pope has opened doors for
dialogue with institutions. What more can we continue to do so that we may continue to feel involved
in this issue?'

'*Laudato si'* is an encyclical on which many hands
worked, and the scientists who worked on it were asked
to say well-founded things and not just set out simple
hypotheses. Many people worked on the encyclical.
My work, in effect, was to set the guidelines, to make
a few corrections and then to prepare the final edition,
yes, with my style and elaborating some things. And
I think we must continue to work, through movements,
academically and also politically. In fact, it is evident
that the world is suffering, not only because of global
warming but because things are being abused and
because nature is being mistreated. One must also bear
in mind, when interpreting *Laudato si'*, that it is not
a "green encyclical". It is a social encyclical. It begins
with the reality of this moment, which is ecological,
but it is a social encyclical. Clearly those who suffer
the consequences are the poorest, those who have been
discarded. It is an encyclical that confronts this culture
of discarding people. We must work hard on the social
part of the encyclical, because the theologians who
worked on it were very concerned to show how much
social impact environmental events can have. And this
is a great help: it should be seen as a social encyclical.'

'Does Pope Francis want a poor Society for the poor? What advice do you give us if we are to walk in that direction?'

'I think that on this point of poverty St Ignatius went far beyond us. When we read how he thought about poverty, and about that vow not to change poverty except to make it more strict, we must reflect. The view of St Ignatius is not just an ascetic attitude, like pinching myself so that it hurts more, but it is a love of poverty as a way of life, as a way of salvation, an ecclesial way. Because for Ignatius, and these are two key words that he uses, poverty is both mother and a bulwark. Poverty nurtures, mothers, generates spiritual life, a life of holiness, apostolic life, and it is a wall, it defends. How many ecclesial disasters began because of a lack of poverty, including outside the Society, I mean in the whole Church in general? How many of the scandals that I, unfortunately, have to find out about, are born of money? I believe that St Ignatius had a very great intuition. In the Ignatian vision of poverty we have a source of inspiration that will help us.

'Clericalism, which is one of the most serious illnesses in the Church, distances itself from poverty. Clericalism is rich. If it is not rich in money, it is rich in pride. But it is rich: in clericalism there is an attachment to possession. It does not allow itself to be nurtured by mother poverty; it does not allow itself to be guarded by the wall of poverty. Clericalism is one of the forms of wealth from which we suffer most seriously in the Church today. At least, in some parts of the Church. Even in the most everyday experiences. The poor Church for the poor is the Church of the Gospel, the Sermon on the Mount in the Gospel of Matthew, and the Sermon on the Plain in the Gospel of Luke, as well as the protocol according to which we will be judged: Matthew 25. I believe that the Gospel is very clear about this, and it is necessary to walk in this direction. But I would also insist that it would be good for the Society to help deepen Ignatius' vision of poverty, because I believe it is a vision for the whole Church. Something that can help us all.'

'You spoke very well of the importance of consolation. When you reflect at the end of each day, what things give you consolation, and what take consolation away from you?'

'I am talking to family, so I can say it: I am rather pessimistic, always! I am not saying that I am depressive, because that is not true. But it is true that I tend to look at the part that did not work well. So for me consolation is the best anti-depressant I have ever found! I find it when I stand before the Lord, and let Him manifest what He has done during the day. When at the end of the day I realize that I am being led, when I realize that, despite my resistance, there has been a driving force carrying me along like a wave, this gives me consolation. It is like feeling, "He is here." With regard to my pontificate, it consoles me to feel within myself: "It was not a convergence of votes that got me into this, but the fact that He is in here." This consoles me. And when I notice the times when my resistances have won, that makes me feel sorrow and leads me to ask for forgiveness. This is quite common ... and it does me good. To realize that, as St Ignatius says, one is "all impediment", to recognize that one has one's resistances and that one experiences them every day and that sometimes one overcomes them and sometimes one does not – this experience stops us getting above our station. This helps us. This is my personal experience, in the simplest possible terms.'

'The apostolic exhortation *Evangelii gaudium* is very inspiring and encourages us to talk more about the theme of evangelization. What do you mean by the last words, in which you exhort us to continue the debate?'

'One of the dangers of the Pope's writings is that they create a little enthusiasm, but then others come along and the preceding ones are filed away. That is why I think it is important to go on working, and hence that final indication that meetings are to be held and the message of *Evangelii gaudium* is to be deepened: it expresses a way of facing different ecclesial problems and evangelization for the Christian life. I think that you were referring to an exhortation that is at the end, and that comes from the *Documento de Aparecida*. In that passage, we wanted to refer to *Evangelii nuntiandi,* which continues to have the freshest timeliness, as it had when it was first published, and that for me remains the most important pastoral document written after Vatican II. But it is not mentioned; it is not cited. Well, the same thing may happen with *Evangelii gaudium*. A few days ago I read that it would be necessary to pick up the point about the homily in *Evangelii gaudium*, because it had passed into silence. This is something that the Church must correct in its preaching, and which takes away a clericalist element. I believe that *Evangelii gaudium* needs to be deepened; it must be worked on by groups of the laity, of priests, in the seminaries, because it is the evangelizing breath that the Church wants to have today. On this we must move forward. It is not something finished, as if we were to say, "That's over, now comes *Laudato si'*." And then, "That's over, too, now it is on to *Amoris laetitia*." By no means! I recommend *Evangelii gaudium* to you as a framework. It is not original, let me be very clear about that. It puts together *Evangelii nuntiandi* and the *Documento de Aparecida*. Although it came after the Synod on Evangelization, the strength of *Evangelii gaudium* was to return to those two documents, to refresh them and to offer them up again on a new plate. *Evangelii gaudium* is the apostolic framework of the Church today.'

'The Church is experiencing a decline in vocations, especially in places where it has been reluctant to promote local vocations.'

'It happened to me more than once in Buenos Aires, as bishop, that very good priests said in conversation with me: "In the parish I have a layman who is worth his weight in gold"! They would describe him as a first-class layman and then ask, "Do you think we can make him a deacon?" This is the problem: the layman who is valuable, we make into a deacon. We clericalize him. In a letter I sent recently to Cardinal Ouellet, I wrote that in Latin America the only thing more or less saved from clericalism is popular piety. In fact, since popular piety is one of those things "of the people" that priests did not believe in, laypeople were creative. Some things may have needed correcting, but popular piety was saved because the priests did not get involved in it. Clericalism does not allow growth; it does not allow the power of baptism to grow. The grace and evangelizing power of missionary expression come from the grace of baptism. And clericalism controls this grace badly and gives rise to dependencies, which sometimes place whole peoples in a state of very great immaturity. I remember the fights that took place when I was a student of theology or a young priest and the base ecclesial communities appeared. Why? Because the laypeople began to have strong leadership, and the first ones who felt insecure were some of the priests. I am generalizing too much, but I do so on purpose: if I caricature the problem, it is because the problem of clericalism is very serious.

'With regard to local vocations, I should say that vocational decline will be discussed at the next Synod. I believe that vocations exist: you just have to know how to propose them and how to attend to them. If the priest is always in a hurry, if he is involved in a thousand administrative things, if we do not convince ourselves that spiritual direction is not a clerical charism but a lay charism (which the priest can also develop) and if we do not call upon the laity in vocational discernment, it is evident that we will have no vocations.

'Young people need to be heard; and the young can be tiring. They always come with the same issues, and you have to listen to them. And of course, for this you have to be patient, to sit down and to listen. And also to be creative: you have to put them to work on things. Today, always having "meetings" no longer makes much sense; they are not fruitful. Young people should be sent on activities that are missionary, catechetical or social, and these do a lot of good.

'Once I visited a parish on the periphery, in a shanty town. The priest had told me he was building a meeting room. And since this priest also taught at the state university, he had aroused enthusiasm and desire among both boys and girls to participate. I arrived on a Saturday, and they were working as masons: the engineer who was running everything was Jewish, one of the girls was an atheist and the other I don't know what, but they were united in a common task. This experience led to the question: can I do something for and with others? You have to put young people to work and listen to them. I would say that these two things are necessary.

'Not promoting local vocations is suicidal. It means nothing less than the sterilization of the Church, because the Church is a mother. Not promoting vocations is an ecclesial tubal ligation. It does not allow that mother to have her children. And that is serious.'

'Digitization is the characteristic feature of this modern age. It creates speed, tension, crises. What is its impact on today's society? How can we have both speed and depth?'

'The Dutch, 30 years or more ago, invented a word: "rapidation". That is, a geometric progression in terms of velocity; and it is this "rapidation" that is turning the digital world into a potential threat. I am not speaking of its positive aspects, because we all know them. I also stress the problem of *liquidity*, which can cancel out what is *concrete*. Someone told me a while ago of a European bishop who went to see a businessman friend. This man showed the bishop how, in ten minutes, he was completing an operation that would make him some profit. From Los Angeles he sold cattle to Hong Kong and in only a few minutes had a profit that was immediately credited to his account. The liquidity of the economy, the liquidity of labour: all of this causes unemployment. And a liquid world. One wants to call for a "return", although I do not like the word because it is a bit nostalgic. "*Volver*" is the title of an Argentinian tango! There is a desire to recover the concrete dimension of work. In Italy 40 per cent of young people aged 25 and under are unemployed; in Spain it is 50 per cent; in Croatia 47 per cent. It is an alarm signal that shows that this liquidity creates unemployment.

'Thank you for your questions and the liveliness of the conversation, and forgive me if I have let my tongue run away with me.'

———

At the end of the dialogue, Fr Arturo Sosa SJ, Superior General of the Society of Jesus, greeted the Pope with these words:

'Holy Father, at the end of these two sessions, on behalf of all the companions gathered in the 36th General Congregation, I want to thank you from my heart for your fraternal presence among us and, thanks be to God, for speaking so freely! Thank you for your contribution to our discernment.

'We are grateful that you have confirmed the invitation to live our charism deeply, walking with the Church and so many men and women of good will, moved by compassion, determined to console by reconciling, sensitive to discern the signs of the times.

'To walk without giving in to the temptation to stay in one of the many beautiful corners we find along the way. To walk, moved by the freedom of the Children of God which makes us available to be sent anywhere, encountering a suffering humanity, following the dynamic of the incarnation of the Lord Jesus, relieving the suffering of so many brothers and sisters, placed, as He was, on the cross.

'We will walk together, according to our way of acting, without dissolving the tensions between faith and justice, dialogue and reconciliation, contemplation and action ... A path that leads us to a deep encounter with the human richness expressed in cultural diversity. We will continue our efforts of inculturation in order to announce the gospel better and to show forth the intercultural face of our common Father.

'We will faithfully follow your advice to join in your unceasing prayer to receive the consolation that will make of each Jesuit, and of all men and women who share the mission of Christ, servants of the joyful news of the Gospel.

'With grateful hearts, we would now like to greet you personally.'

7

Take the Gospel Without Tranquillizers: A conversation with the Superiors General

'The Pope is late', they tell me at the entrance to the Vatican's Paul VI Audience Hall on 26 November 2016. Inside, in the place where Synods are held, 140 Superiors General of the Male Religious Orders and Congregations (USG) are waiting. They are gathered at the end of their 88th General Assembly. Outside there is a little light rain. 'The Fruitfulness of the Prophetic in Religious Life' was the theme of the Assembly, which had met on 23–5 November at the House of the Salesians in Rome.

It is not often that the Pope is late. At 10.15 the photographers arrive, and then, quickly and decisively, the Pope. After the welcoming applause, Francis begins: 'Sorry for the delay. Life is like this: full of surprises. Thank you so much.' And he goes on saying that he does not want his lateness to lessen the time fixed for us to be together. So the meeting lasts a full three hours and finishes at around 1.15.

Halfway through the meeting there is a pause of about 30 minutes. A small room had been set aside for the Pope, but he said: 'Why do you want to leave me on my own?' And so he joyfully spent the break with the religious superiors taking a coffee and a snack and greeting people.

No talk had been prepared beforehand either by the Pope or by the religious. The CTV cameras only recorded the initial greetings and then retired. The meeting had to be free and fraternal, comprising questions and unfiltered answers. The Pope did not want to read the questions beforehand. After a very brief greeting from Fr Mario Johri, general minister of the Capuchin Friars and president of the USG, and its general secretary, Fr David Glenday, Combonian, the Pope took questions from the Assembly.

And if there were criticisms? 'It is good to be criticized,' the Pope affirms, 'I like it, always. Life also includes misunderstandings and tensions. And when they are criticisms that make us grow, I accept them, I respond. But the hardest questions do not come from the religious. They come from young people. They put you on the spot, they certainly do. Lunches with the young people at the World Youth Days or other occasions have put me to the test. They are so open and sincere and they ask the most awkward questions. Now you, ask your questions!'

'Holy Father, we recognize your ability to speak to young people and ignite in them a love for the cause of the Gospel. We know of your commitment to drawing young people to the Church; for this you have convoked the next Synod of Bishops on youth, faith and vocational discernment. What motivated you to convoke the Synod on youth? What should we do to reach them today?'

'At the end of the last Synod each participant gave three suggestions for the theme of the next one. Then the episcopal conferences were consulted. There was convergence on the main themes such as young people, training of priests, inter-religious dialogue and peace. In the first post-Synod Council a great discussion took place. I was there. I always go, but I don't speak. For me the important thing really is to listen. I need to listen, I let them work freely. This way I understand how the issues arise, what the proposals and difficulties are, and how they are confronted.

'They chose young people. But some underlined the importance of the training of priests. Personally, I am very keen on the theme of discernment. I have often recommended it to the Jesuits: in Poland and then to the General Congregation. Discernment brings together the issues of formation of the young for life: for youth, particularly, and especially seminarians and future pastors. Training and accompaniment to the priesthood need discernment.

'At the moment this is one of the greatest problems that we have in the education of priests. In education we are used to formulas, to black and white, but not to the grey areas of life. And what counts is life, not formulas. We need to grow in discernment. The logic of black and white can lead to casuistic abstraction. Instead, discernment means going beyond the grey areas of life according to God's will. And you look for God's will by following the true doctrine of the Gospel and not in the fixity of an abstract doctrine. Reflecting on the education of young people and on the training of seminarians, I decided the final theme as it has been announced: "Youth, Faith and Vocational Discernment".

The Church must accompany young people in their journey to maturity, and only through discernment and not with abstractions can they discover their project of life and live in a manner truly open to God and to the world. So I chose this theme to introduce discernment as a more powerful force in the life of the Church. The other day we had our second meeting of the post-Synod Council. This area was discussed at length. They have prepared a first draft on the *Lineamenta* that will be sent to the Episcopal Conferences straight away. Religious have also worked on it. A good draft has been produced.

'This, however, is the key point: discernment is always dynamic, as is life. Static things don't work, especially for young people. When I was young, the fashion was to have meetings. Today, static things like meetings are no good. We have to work with young people doing things, working, with missions to the people, social work, going every week to give food to the homeless. Young people find the Lord in action. Then, after the action, we need to have some reflection. But reflecting on its own is not a help: they are ideas … just ideas. So two words: listening and movement. This is important. But not only to train young people to listen, but rather and above all to listen to them, to young people themselves. This is a first very important task for the Church: listen to young people. And in preparing the Synod the presence of the religious is truly important, for the religious work a lot with young people.'

'What do you expect from the religious life in preparing for the Synod? What hopes do you have for the next Synod on young people, in light of the diminishing strength of religious life in the West?'

'Certainly it is true that there is a diminution in the forces of religious life in the West. This is connected to demographic issues. But it is also true that vocational pastoral care does not respond to the needs of young people. The next Synod will give us ideas. The shrinking of religious life in the West worries me.

'Something else worries me: the rise of new religious Institutes, which raise some concerns. I am not saying there is no need for new religious Institutes! But in some cases I wonder what is happening today. Some of them appear to be something very new, they seem to express a great apostolic force, they draw in many people, and then ... they collapse. Sometimes scandalous things are discovered behind them ... There are some new small foundations that are really good and do things seriously. I see that behind these good foundations there are sometimes groups of bishops who accompany them and ensure their growth. But there are others that are born not from a charism of the Holy Spirit but from human charisma, from charismatic people who attract others by their appealing human skills. Some are, I could say, "restorationists": they appear to provide safety, and instead they offer only rigidity. When I am told that there is a Congregation that attracts many vocations, I confess that I am worried. The Spirit does not work with the logic of human success: the Spirit has another way. But they say to me: there are many young people committing themselves, praying a great deal, they are very faithful. And I say to myself: "Very well: we'll see if it is the Lord!"

'Some of them are Pelagians: they want to return to ascesis, they do penance, they seem to be soldiers ready to do anything to defend the faith and good practices ... and then the scandal of the founder or foundress explodes. We don't know, do we? Jesus' style is different. The Holy Spirit made a noise on the day of Pentecost: that was the beginning. Usually the Spirit does not make so much noise, but carries a cross. The Holy Spirit is not triumphalist. God's style is the cross that is carried forward until the Lord says "Enough". Triumphalism does not go well with the consecrated life.

'So, do not put your hope in the sudden and powerful flowering of these Institutes. Seek instead the humble path of Jesus, that of evangelical witness. Benedict XVI told us rightly: the Church grows not by proselytizing but by attraction.'

'Why did you choose three Marian themes for the next three World Youth Days that will lead to the World Days of Panama?'

'I didn't choose them! From Latin America they asked for a strong Marian presence. It is true that Latin America is very Marian, and that struck me as a very good thing. I did not receive any other proposals and I was happy with this one. But the true Madonna! Not the Madonna in charge of a post office who sends out a letter every day saying, "My child, do this and then the next day do that." No, not this. The true Madonna is the one who generates Jesus in our hearts, as a mother. The trend of the superstar Madonna, who puts herself at the centre as a protagonist, is not Catholic.'

'Holy Father, your mission in the Church is not an easy one. In spite of the challenges, the tensions, the opposition, you offer us the witness of a man of serenity, a man at peace. What is the source of this serenity? What is the source of the trust that inspires you and sustains you in your mission? Called to be religious guides, what do you suggest we do to live out our tasks responsibly and in peace?'

'What is the source of my serenity? No, I don't take tranquillizers! The Italians offer a good piece of advice: to live in peace you need a healthy dose of indifference. I have no problem saying that what I am living through is a completely new experience for me. In Buenos Aires I was more anxious, I admit. I felt more tense and worried. Indeed: I was not like I am now. I have had a very particular experience of peace since the moment I was elected. And it has not left me. I live in peace. I can't explain it.

'As for the conclave, they tell me that the London bookmakers put me at number 42 or 46. I did not foresee it at all. I even had my homily ready for Holy Thursday. In the newspapers they said I was a king-maker, but not the Pope. At the moment of the election I simply said: "Lord, let's move forward!" I felt peace, and that peace has never left me.

'In the general congregations we spoke about the problems in the Vatican, about reform. Everybody wanted it. There is corruption in the Vatican. But I am at peace. If there is a problem, I write a note to St Joseph and I put it under a little statue in my room. It is the statue of St Joseph sleeping. And now he is sleeping on a mattress of notes! That is why I sleep well: it is a grace of God. I always sleep for six hours.

And I pray. I pray in my own way. The breviary is very dear to me, and I never leave it. Mass every day. The rosary ... When I pray, I always take the Bible. And peace grows. I don't know if this is the secret ... My peace is a gift from the Lord. Let it not be taken away!

'I think each of us has to find the root of the choice that the Lord has made for us. Besides, losing your peace of mind doesn't help you to cope with suffering. The superiors need to learn how to suffer, but to suffer as a father. And also to suffer with great humility. This is the road to go, from the cross to peace. Never wash your hands of problems! Yes, in the Church there are Pontius Pilates who wash their hands of things in order to be at peace. But a superior who washes his hands is not a father and does not help.'

'Holy Father, you have often told us that the specific characteristic of the religious life is prophecy. We have looked at length at what it means to be radical in prophecy. What are the safety zones and comfort zones from which we are called to break out? You spoke to the nuns of a "prophetic and credible ascesis". How do you understand this in renewed terms? How can the consecrated life contribute to a culture of mercy?'

'Being radical in prophecy. This is very important to me. I'll take Joel 3 as an "icon". It often comes to mind and I know it comes from God. It says: "The elders shall dream dreams and the young shall prophesy." That verse is a linchpin for the spirituality of the generations. Being radical in prophecy is the famous *sine glossa*, the rule *sine glossa*, the Gospel *sine glossa*. That is: without tranquillizers. The Gospel should be taken without tranquillizers. This is what our founders did.

'The radicalism of our prophecy must be sought in our founders. They remind us that we are called to leave our comfort zones and our safety, all that is worldly: in the way we live, and also in thinking out new avenues for our Institutes. New roads need to be sought in the foundational charism and in the initial prophecy. We need to recognize personally and as a community what our worldliness is.

'Even the ascetic can be worldly. But instead they need to be prophetic. When I entered the novitiate of the Jesuits, they gave me the *cilice*.[1] The *cilice* is good, but be careful: it is not there to help me show me how good and strong I am. True ascesis must make me freer. I think fasting is something that is still used: but how do I fast? Simply not eating? St Theresa of Lisieux had another way: never saying what she liked. She never complained and she accepted everything that was given to her. There is a daily ascesis, a small ascesis, that is a constant mortification. A phrase of St Ignatius comes to mind, one that helps us to be free and happy. He said that, to follow the Lord, mortification in all possible things helps. If something helps you, do it, even the *cilice*! But only if it helps you to be more free, not if you need it to show yourself that you are strong.'

'What does community life entail? What is the role of a superior in keeping this prophecy? How can the religious contribute to the renewal of structures and mentality of the Church?'

'Community life? Some saints defined it as a continual penance. There are communities where people fight like cats and dogs! If mercy does not enter the community, things are not good. For the religious, the ability to forgive often must begin within the community. And this is prophetic. You start with listening: let everybody feel they are being heard. Superiors need to listen and persuade. If superiors constantly rebuke, it does not help to create the radical prophecy of the religious life. I am convinced that religious have an advantage in making a contribution to the renewal of the structures and the mentality of the Church.

'In the Presbyteral Councils in the dioceses the religious help in the process. And they should not be afraid to make themselves heard. A worldly, princely climate can enter the structures of the Church, and the religious must contribute to destroying this evil climate. And you don't need to become a cardinal to think of yourself as a prince! It is enough to be clerical. This is what is worst in the organization of the Church. The religious can bear witness like an inverted iceberg, with the top at the base.'

'Holy Father, we hope that through your guidance better relations may develop between the consecrated life and the particular Churches. What do you suggest to us so that we may fully express our charisms in the particular Churches and face the difficulties that sometimes arise in relations with the bishops and the diocesan clergy? How do you see dialogue between the religious life and the bishops and collaboration with the local Church?'

'For some time there has been a desire to revise the criteria for the relations between the bishops and the religious established in 1978 by the Congregation for Religious and the Congregation for Bishops with the document *Mutuae relationes*. This was already discussed in the Synod of 1994. That document was a response to a certain period and is no longer up to date. It is time for a change.

'It is important that the religious feel they are fully part of the diocesan Church. Fully. Sometimes there are many misunderstandings that do not aid unity, and so there is a need to give a name to these problems. The religious must be in the structures of governance of the local Church: administrative councils, Presbyteral Councils ... In Buenos Aires the religious elected their representatives to the Presbyteral Council. The work should be shared among the structures of the diocese. You cannot help one another from a position of isolation. There must be a lot of growth in this. And it helps the bishop not to fall into the temptation of becoming a little prince.

'And spirituality needs to be spread and shared too, and the religious carry powerful spiritual currents. In some dioceses the secular clergy gather together in different spiritual groups, Franciscans, Carmelites ... And the very style of living needs to be shared; some diocesan priests ask if they can live together so as not to be alone, to have a bit of community life. The desire comes, for example, when there is the good witness of a parish followed by a religious community. So, there is a level of radical collaboration, because it is spiritual, from the soul. And being close together spiritually within a diocese between the religious and the clergy helps to resolve some possible misunderstandings. You can study and rethink many things. These include the length of service as a parish priest, which seems to me to be too short, and parish priests are changed too easily.'

'Holy Father, like the Church, the religious life is committed to facing up to situations of sexual abuse of minors and financial abuse with transparency and determination. All of this is a counter-testimony, it causes scandals and has repercussions at the level of vocations and the help of benefactors. What measures do you suggest to prevent such scandals within our Congregations?'

'Perhaps there isn't time for a very detailed response, and I have confidence in your wisdom. But let me say that the Lord wants the religious to be poor. When they are not poor, the Lord sends a finance officer to push the Institute into bankruptcy! Sometimes religious congregations are accompanied by administrators who are "friends" but who lead you into bankruptcy. Anyhow, the fundamental criteria for a finance officer is that they are not personally attached to money. Once it happened that a sister who ran the finances fainted and a fellow religious said to those aiding her: "Wave a banknote under her nose, she'll soon come round!" This makes us laugh, but also think. We also need to check how the banks are investing the money. They must never be invested in weapons, for example. Never.

'Concerning sexual abuse: it seems that out of every four people who are abused, two will later go on to abuse. The seeds of future abuse are planted like that: it is devastating. If priests or religious are involved, it is clear that the devil is at work, destroying the work of Jesus through those who should be proclaiming Jesus. But let's be clear: this is a sickness. If we do not think it is a sickness, we can never treat the problem. So be careful in receiving candidates to the religious life for formation without properly assessing their adequate level of emotional maturity. For example: never receive to the religious life or to a diocese candidates who have been rejected from another seminary or another Institute without asking for clear and detailed information on their reasons for leaving.'

'Holy Father, the religious life is not an end in itself; its purpose is its mission in the world. You invited us to be a Church that is outgoing. From your vantage point, is the religious life around the world carrying out this mission?'

'The Church was born going out. She was shut in the Upper Room, and then she went out. And she must continue to be outgoing. She shouldn't go back to hiding in the Upper Room. This is what Jesus wanted. And by "out", I mean to the peripheries, both existential and social. The existential poor and the social poor push the Church beyond herself. Let us think of one form of poverty, the one tied to the problem of migrants and refugees: the lives of those people are more important than international agreements! And it is in the very service of charity that you can find great terrain for ecumenical dialogue: it is the poor who unite the divided Christians! These are all the challenges open for the religious of a Church that is going out. The *Evangelii gaudium*, the Joy of the Gospel, seeks to share this necessity: go out! I would like you to go back to that apostolic exhortation with reflection and prayer. It has matured in the light of the *Evangelii nuntiandi* and the work done at [the shrine of our Lady of] Aparecida and contains a wide-reaching ecclesial reflection. And in the end we recall it always: God's mercy is outgoing. And God is always merciful. And you too, go out!'

At around 1 p.m. the meeting concluded with some words of thanks and lengthy applause. The Pope, already standing, before leaving the Aula, greeted all with these words:

'Go on with courage and without fear of error! Those who never make mistakes are those who never do anything. We must go forward! We will get things wrong, sometimes, yes, but there is always the mercy of God on our side!' And before leaving the Hall, Francis wanted to greet once again all those present, one by one.

8

GRACE IS NOT AN IDEOLOGY: POPE FRANCIS'S PRIVATE CONVERSATION WITH SOME COLOMBIAN JESUITS

Antonio Spadaro SJ

From 6 to 11 September 2017 Pope Francis was in Colombia, completing his 20th apostolic visit. The voyage included a visit on 10 September to the city of Cartagena de Indias, the capital of the region of Bolívar that looks onto the Caribbean Sea to the north of Colombia.

The Pope went first to St Francis of Assisi Square, and then went on to the sanctuary of St Peter Claver, greeting people along the way. After reciting the Angelus in the square, he entered the sanctuary and remained in silence some moments before the altar that contains the relics of the saint, laying some flowers that had been given to him by two children.

Some 300 representatives of the Afro-Colombian community served by the Jesuits were in the church. The Pope gave a gift to the rector of the sanctuary.

Afterwards he went into the inner courtyard, where he met privately with representatives of the community of the Society of Jesus, made up of 65 religious.

Francis was welcomed with song and applause. Then he sat down and gave thanks for the meeting. Referring to the Society of Jesus, he said playfully, 'I like meeting with the sect', prompting laughter all round.

'Thank you for what you are doing in Colombia', he said, and continued: 'Yesterday I was very happy to meet Álvaro Restrepo in Medellín. He was the Provincial in Argentina. He used to come to my residence to talk ... He's a great man, very good, very good. Well, I am here for you. I don't want to make a speech, if you have some questions or something you want to know, ask me now, that's best: provoke and inspire me!'

Somebody immediately asked for a blessing, but the Pope replied: 'At the end. When I give my concluding blessing, I'll bless you all.'

Fr Carlos Eduardo Correa SJ, the Jesuit Provincial in Colombia, announced: 'Dear Pope Francis, we are very happy because your message in these days in Colombia has encouraged us in the commitment to reconciliation and peace. We want to say to you that in all our work we want to continue taking these processes forward, so that in this country we can live the fellowship of the Gospel, and for this we want to thank you from our hearts for encouraging us and confirming us in the faith and in hope. Sincere thanks and may God continue to bless your ministry.' Francis thanked him for his words.

After the Provincial came the rector of the 'Javeriana' Pontifical University, Fr Jorge Humberto Peláez SJ: 'Your Holiness, this has been a marvellous gift because Colombia has sunk into a state of despair. With this visit we will take not just one step forward but many. You can count on the Javeriana University and the entire educational and pastoral work of the Jesuits for the work of reconciliation. Thank you for this visit. It gives us hope, Your Holiness.'

Fr Jorge Iván Moreno asked the first question: 'Dear Francis, I'm pastor of the parish of St Rita. The people there love you and appreciate you, and we wrote you a letter a few days ago. I want to know: when you were in San Francisco at those communities at Pie de la Popa, what struck you most? I think it's the first time you've been to Cartagena and I'd like to know: as Pontiff, what have you seen while passing through this "other" Cartagena, as we call it?'

His Holiness replied: 'Let's stop at the question, as I think it gives me an opportunity to say something very dear to me. What I noticed and what touched me most was the spontaneity. The people of God there placed no limits on their joyful enthusiasm. Scholars could give a thousand different interpretations, but it was simply the people of God going out to be welcoming.

OPEN TO GOD: OPEN TO THE WORLD

'For me there was a clear indication that this wasn't something prepared beforehand with ready-made slogans: the very culture of these different parts of the people of God, these areas I passed through, expressed itself in complete freedom, praising God. It's unusual.

'Sadly, we are often tempted to evangelize *for* the people, *towards* the people, but *without* the people of God. Everything for the people, but nothing with the people. This way of being, in the final analysis, is due to a liberal and illuminist vision of evangelization. Surely, the first rejection of such a vision comes in *Lumen gentium*: the Church is the holy people of God. So, if we want to hear the Church, we have to hear the people of God. People ... today we need to be careful when we speak of people! For someone might say: "You'll end up being populists", and they'll start concocting theories.

'But we need to understand that this "people" is not a category in logic. If you want to speak of people with logical schemes, you end up falling into an illuminist and liberal ideology, or a "populist" one, right ... anyway you end up closing the people into an ideological schema. "People", however, refers to a *mythical* category. And to understand the people we need to immerse ourselves in them, we need to accompany them from within.

'To be a Church, the holy pilgrim people, faithful to God, requires pastors who let themselves be carried forward by the reality of the people, which is not a mere ideology: it is vital, it is alive. The grace of God that is present in the life of the people is not an ideology. Certainly, many theologians could explain several important things that need to be known about the theme. But I want to say that grace is not an ideology: it is an embrace, it is something bigger.

'When I come to places like Cartagena, where people express themselves freely, I see they are expressing themselves as the people of God. Certainly, it is true that some say that the people are superstitious.

'So I tell them to go and read Paul VI, who in *Evangelii nuntiandi*, n. 48, highlighted the risks involved but also the virtues of the people. He said that popular piety is, yes, open to the penetration of superstition. But he also said that, if it is well ordered, then it is full of values and shows a thirst for God that only the simple and the poor can know. The people of God have a good sense of smell. Perhaps the people struggle to communicate well, and sometimes people get it wrong ... But can any of us say, "Thank you, Lord, for I have never been wrong?" No.

'The people of God have a good sense of smell. And sometimes our task as pastors is to be behind the people. A pastor has to take up all three positions: in front to mark out the road, in the middle, to know it, and at the back to ensure nobody falls behind and to let the flock seek the road ... and the sheep smell a good pasture. A pastor has to move continually between these three positions. See, this is what your question has prompted me to say.'

'Good evening, your Holiness. I am Rodolfo Abello, responsible for youth work in the province. I want to ask something along these lines: towards which horizon should we be encouraging our young people with Ignatian spirituality?'

'What comes to me is to say something a bit intellectual: put them into the spirituality of the *Exercises*. What do I mean? I mean, set them in motion, put them into action. Youth work as pure reflection in small groups no longer works today. This pastoral approach to inactive youth gets no traction. You have to make them move: whether they are practising or non-practising, you need to get them up and active.

'If they are believers, leading them will be easy. If they are non-believers, you need to let life itself make demands of them, but in action and with accompaniment. Impose nothing, accompany them ... in volunteering, working with the elderly, in teaching basic literacy ... all appropriate activities for young people. If we put a young person into action, we facilitate a dynamic where the Lord starts to speak and move the heart of that person. It won't be for us to stir the heart with our wisdom; at best we can help by using our minds once the heart moves.

'Yesterday at Medellín I recalled an event that was very important to me because it came from the heart. At Kraków during lunch with the archbishop and 15 young people from around the world – there is such a lunch at every World Youth Day – they started to ask questions and a dialogue opened up.

'A university student asked me: "Some of my companions are atheists, what do I have to say to persuade them?" I noticed a sense of ecclesial militancy in the young man. The response came to me clearly: "The last thing to do is to use words, really, speaking is the very last thing. Start by acting, invite him along, and when he sees what you do and how you do it, then he will ask you, and then you can start to speak."

'What I am saying is to get young people moving, invent things that make them feel as though they are the protagonists and then lead them to ask themselves: "What is happening, what has changed my heart, why does this make me happy?" Just as in the *Exercises* when considering interior movements. Obviously, though, don't ask young people what movements they have experienced because they won't understand your language.

'But let them tell you how they feel, and from there engage with them bit by bit. To do this – and here's a tip I received from the much-loved Fr Furlong when they made me Provincial – you need to have the patience to sit and listen to those who come asking questions, and you need to know how to handle people who want to push you into endless discussions. Young people are tiring, young people are discussing, so you need this continual mortification of being among them to listen, always and in any way. But for me the key point is the movement.'

The Jesuit scholastic Jefferson Chaverra put this request to the Pope: 'Your Holiness, first, I want to thank you for coming to visit us and for coming to Colombia. Second, I don't want to ask a real question but to make a request in the name of all Afro-Colombians, of all the black people of Colombia. I want to thank you for the many priests and bishops committed to our causes and at the same time tell you, and in your name tell the whole Church, that we blacks in Colombia need greater accompaniment by and engagement with the Church, for our pain and our suffering as black people continue to be enormous, and the workers are still few. Your Holiness, the harvest is great but the labourers are few.'

'What you say is true. I spoke of this matter you touch on in my talk to the bishops. There is a basic charism for the Colombian Jesuit: a person whose name is Peter Claver. I believe that God has spoken to us through this man. This impresses me. He was just a weak boy, a young Jesuit doing his training, yet he spoke so much to the old porter. And the old man nourished his aspirations. How good it would be if the elderly in our society were to step forward and the youth follow them: this would fulfil the words of Joel: "The elderly will dream and the young will prophesy." And so there is a need to prophesy, and to speak with the elderly.'

Fr Jorge Alberto Camacho, pastor of the St Peter Claver parish, said to the Pope: 'Holiness, real thanks to you for being here with us. You have made a present to the sanctuary, and we from the sanctuary want to reciprocate with some small tokens. One is the process of canonization of St Peter Claver. It contains everything that made him a saint, his actions that enable us to work, like you. Fr Tulio Aristizábal, the eldest member of our community in Cartagena, is 96 and an expert on St Peter Claver. He will give you the book.'

Fr Aristizábal stood up and, with great emotion, said: 'My father superior has asked me to give you as a gift the book of the process of canonization of St Peter Claver. It contains a most interesting section: the sworn declaration of more than 30 slaves who tell us about St Peter. In my mind, this is the best biography of the saint. I place it in your hands.' Pope Francis thanked him.

Fr Jorge Alberto Camacho continued: 'Holiness, the other present we have prepared for you is a programme we have been promoting these past three months. We have called it the Pope Francis Ruta Verde, or Green Way. It takes the encyclical *Laudato*

Si' into the popular districts. As a sign of this way, we want to give you the booklet that we have used with the youngsters in the streets and the T-shirt of the Ruta Verde. At the end we will ask Your Holiness to bless these objects and the saplings of the Ruta Verde, local fruit trees that we have planted in the city.'

Fr Vicente Durán Casas stood to ask another question: 'Holy Father, again thank you for your visit. I teach philosophy and I would like to know, and I speak for my teaching colleagues in theology too, what do you expect from philosophical and theological reflection in a country such as ours, and in the Church generally?'

'To start, I'd say let's not have laboratory reflection. We've seen what damage occurred when the great and brilliant Thomist scholastics deteriorated, falling down, down, down to a mechanistic scholasticism without life, mere ideas that transformed into a casuistic pastoral approach. At least, in our day we were trained that way ... I'd say it was quite ridiculous how, to explain metaphysical continuity, the philosopher Losada spoke of *puncta inflata* ... To demonstrate some ideas, things got ridiculous. He was a good philosopher, but decadent, he didn't become famous.

'So, philosophy not in a laboratory, but in life, in dialogue with reality. In dialogue with reality, philosophers will find the three transcendentals that constitute unity, but they will have a real name. Recall the words of our great writer Dostoevsky. Like him, we must reflect on what sort of beauty will save us, on goodness, on truth. Benedict XVI spoke of truth as an encounter – that is to say, no longer a classification, but a road. Always in dialogue with reality, for you cannot do philosophy with a logarithmic table.

'The same is true for theology, but this does not mean to corrupt theology, depriving it of its purity. Quite the opposite. The theology of Jesus was the most real thing of all; it began with reality and rose up to the Father. It began with a seed, a parable, a fact ... and explained them. Jesus wanted to construct a deep theology, and the great reality is the Lord. I like to repeat that, to be a good theologian, together with study you have to be dedicated, awake and seize hold of reality; and you need to reflect on all of this on your knees.

'A man who does not pray, a woman who does not pray, cannot be a theologian. They might be a living form of Denzinger, they might know every possible existing doctrine, but they'll not be doing theology. They'll be a compendium or a manual containing everything. But today it is a matter of how you express God, how you say who God is, how you show the Spirit, the wounds of Christ, the mystery of Christ, starting with the Letter to the Philippians 2:7. How you explain these mysteries and keep explaining them, and how you teach the encounter that is grace.

As when you read Paul in the Letter to the Romans, where there's the entire mystery of grace and you want to explain it.

'I'll use this question to say something else that I believe should be said out of justice, and also out of charity. In fact, I hear many comments – they are respectable for they come from children of God, but wrong – concerning the post-Synod apostolic exhortation. To understand *Amoris laetitia* you need to read it all the way from the beginning to the end. Start with the first chapter, and then go on to the second and so on … and reflect. And read what was said in the Synod.

'A second thing: some maintain that there is no Catholic morality underlying *Amoris laetitia*, or at least, no sure morality. I want to repeat clearly that the morality of *Amoris laetitia* is Thomist, the morality of the great Thomas. You can talk about it with a great theologian. One of the best today and one of the most mature is Cardinal Schönborn.

'I want to say this so that you can help those who believe that morality is purely casuistic. Help them understand that the great Thomas possesses the greatest richness, which is still able to inspire us today. But on your knees, always on your knees.'

Before leaving, the Holy Father blessed the Jesuits, asking them not to forget to pray for him.

9

AT THE CROSSROADS OF HISTORY: CONVERSATIONS WITH THE JESUITS IN MYANMAR AND BANGLADESH

From 26 November to 2 December 2017 Pope Francis travelled to Myanmar and Bangladesh on his 21st international apostolic journey. On Wednesday, 29 November, following his encounter with the bishops of Myanmar, Francis left the small room that had hosted the meeting and found himself before 300 seminarians who were waiting for a photo opportunity. He also greeted a small group of Chinese people proudly waving the flag of the People's Republic. Their words were 'Come to our country soon!'

After walking among these joyful gatherings, the Pope entered the chapel on the ground floor of the archbishop's house to meet 31 Jesuits based in the country: 13 were from Myanmar (three priests, five novices and five scholastics); the others were from Thailand, Malaysia, Vietnam, India, Indonesia, Australia and China. Another 21 Myanmar Jesuits were not present because they were studying in Indonesia, Sri Lanka and the Philippines.

Collectively, those present represented all the institutions of the Society of Jesus in the country: educational institutions that are open to all, regardless of ethnic or religious background; a parish in a border diocese serving the Kachin and Shan people; a school in a slum area in Yangon, where Jesuits also help the poor to rebuild their homes and have a small micro-credit service; and the Jesuit Refugee Service, which mostly works with hundreds of thousands of displaced people in the Kachin and Kayah states and on the border with Thailand and China.

Upon entering, Francis was welcomed with applause, and then he proceeded to greet everyone individually. As is typical of a chapel, the room was narrow and long, but the atmosphere was that of a spontaneous embrace breaking through the chairs, set in rows. The faces of those present made it clear that the Pope was in the company of people with many different roots and backgrounds. A Jesuit student placed around his shoulders a shawl typical of the Chin ethnic group.

Francis sat down and said he needed an English translator, promptly presenting Monsignor Mark Miles. Jokingly, the Pope added, 'He is a good man and will not reveal any of the Jesuit secrets we talk about here.' And then he spontaneously thanked those present.

What follows is a transcript of the two conversations I attended, the publication of which has been approved by the Holy Father. Accompanying the text are some background notes to contextualize the conversation and a final consideration.

Antonio Spadaro SJ

'Thank you for coming. I see many young faces, and I'm glad. It's a good thing, because it's a promise. Young people have a future if they have roots. If they do not have roots, they will be at the mercy of the wind. To begin with, I would like to ask a question. Everyone should ask it in their examination of conscience: where are my roots? Do I have roots? Are my roots tenacious or weak? It is a question that does us good. St Ignatius began the *Spiritual Exercises* speaking of a root: "Humans are created to praise." And he concluded with another root: the root of love. And he proposed a contemplation to grow in love. There is no true love if it does not take root. There it is; that was my initial sermon! But now I would like you to ask a few questions.'

'Thank you, Holy Father, for being with us. We all live in Myanmar, and you understand the situation in our country. We share the same spirituality, that of the *Spiritual Exercises*. Our spirituality contemplates the Incarnation, which pushes us forward; it moves us to mission. We are here, and therefore we are on a mission. Contemplating the actual situation in Myanmar, what do you expect from us?'

'I believe we cannot think of a mission – I say this not only as a Jesuit but as a Christian – without the mystery of the Incarnation. The mystery of the Incarnation illuminates our approach to reality and the world completely, all our closeness to people, to culture. Christian closeness is always incarnated. It is a closeness like that of the word, who comes to be with us. I remind you of the *synkatabasis,* the being with … The Jesuit is one who must always get closer, as the Word made flesh came close. To look, to listen without prejudices, but mystically. To look without fear and look mystically: this is fundamental for the way we look at reality.

'Inculturation begins with this way of looking. Inculturation is not a fashion, no. It is the very essence of the Word which became flesh, took our culture, our language, our flesh, our life, and died. Inculturation is taking on board the culture of the people I am sent to.

'And for this reason the Jesuit prayer – I mean mainly in relation to inculturation – is the prayer of intercession. It is necessary to pray to the Lord precisely for those realities in which I am immersed.

'There have been many failures in the Society's life of prayer. At first some Jesuits gave St Ignatius a headache because they wanted the Jesuits to remain shut away and to dedicate two or three hours to prayer ... And St Ignatius said, "No, contemplate in action!" And in 1974 it was my turn to experience this. There was – as you know – a movement of the so-called "Discalced Jesuits", who wanted a rigid, almost cloistered observance of the rules. A contrary reform, against the spirit of St Ignatius. True prayer and true Jesuit observance do not follow that route. It is not a restorationist observance. Our observance is always to look forward with the inspiration of the past, but always looking forward. The challenges are not behind; they lie ahead.

'For this, Blessed Pope Paul VI helped the Society greatly, and on 3 December 1974 he addressed us with a speech that remains entirely relevant. I recommend you read it. He makes, for example, a remark: "Wherever, at the crossroads of history, there are Jesuits."[1] Paul VI said it! He did not say, "Be locked up in a convent", but he told the Jesuits, "Go to the crossroads!" And to go to the crossroads of history, my dear friends, we must pray! We must be men of prayer alive in the crossroads of history!'

'I would like to reflect for a moment on our people. Some here have walked three days to see you; others have put money aside for six months. I can testify that they were happy to see you. Thank you! My question is this: many in the media have said that your visit to Myanmar is one of your most difficult and is full of challenges. Is it as they suggest?'

'You said two things. First you talked about the People of God. When I heard that these people had travelled and walked a lot, that they had saved money to come here, I confess that I felt a great sense of shame. The People of God teach us heroic virtues. And I feel ashamed at being a shepherd of a people who overtake me in their virtue, in their thirst for God, their sense of belonging to the Church, their desire to come to see Peter. I felt it, and I thank God for letting me feel it. And incidentally I tell you that, if there is a grace that the Jesuit must ask for, it is shame, great shame. St Ignatius tells us to ask for it in the First Week of the *Spiritual Exercises* before the Crucified Christ. Ask for the grace of shame, for you and for me. It is a grace!

'Let me now turn to your second question. This is a very difficult journey, yes. Perhaps it even risked being cancelled at some point. So it is a difficult journey. But precisely because it is difficult, I had to make it! In fact, a short time ago we read in the Office of Readings what the prophet Ezekiel says of the pastors who take advantage of their people, who live off their people. They live to suck their milk; they are shepherds who take the milk from the sheep and shear their wool. Here are two symbols. Food stands for riches, and wool for vanity. A pastor who becomes accustomed to riches and vanity ends up, as St Ignatius says, suffering great pride. Hence St Augustine takes up this theme of the prophet Ezekiel in a famous treatise, *De pastoribus*, and shows that if the bad shepherd clings to wealth, if he clings to vanity, he ends up becoming full of pride. So, what makes the good shepherd healthy is poverty. St Ignatius called poverty the mother and the bulwark of religious life. The People of God are a poor people, a humble people and a people who thirst for God. We pastors must learn from the people. So, if this journey seemed difficult, I came because we have to be at the crossroads of history.'

'When we heard about your visit, we began to feel and think that we were at the crossroads, as you just said. Your visit for us is a push forward in this sense. The key is, as you often say, to have the smell of the sheep upon us. We come here from different places in Myanmar, where we perceive this smell as priests. Some of us smell the refugees. How can we feel and think with the Church, as St Ignatius asks us, sensing this smell of the People of God so intensely? How can we feel the presence of the Pope?'

'I recently spoke to the bishops about two smells: the smell of the sheep and the smell of God. We must know the smell of sheep, to acknowledge, understand and accompany, and the sheep must perceive that we exude the smell of God. And this is the testimony. Today, the missionary activity, thanks be to God, is not a matter of proselytism. Pope Benedict XVI made it clear: the Church grows not by proselytism but by attraction, by witness. How can you feel the presence of the Pope, you who work there? How can refugees feel it? Answering is not easy. I have visited four refugee camps so far. Three huge ones in Lampedusa, Lesbos and Bologna, which is in northern Italy. There our work is of closeness. Sometimes it is not possible to distinguish well between a place one person expects to leave and a prison under another name. And sometimes the camps are nothing other than concentration camps, prisons.

'In Italy, the presence of refugees from Africa is strongly felt, because they are there, so close, and real tragedies happen. A refugee I spoke to told me that it took him three years to get from his house to Lampedusa. And in those three years he was sold five times. On the trafficking of young women, girls who are deceived and sold to traffickers in Rome, an elderly priest once told me with a certain irony, that he was not sure if there were more priests in Rome or young women enslaved in prostitution. And they are girls who have been kidnapped, deceived, carried from one place to another. The diocesan Church of Rome works a lot on this issue. It is a work of liberation.

'Then we think about the exploitation of children forced into child labour. We think of children who have forgotten how to play. They have to work. Here is our Third Week of the *Spiritual Exercises* of St Ignatius: to see them is to see Christ suffering and crucified. How do I approach all this? Yes, I try to visit,

I speak clearly, especially with countries that have closed their borders. Unfortunately, in Europe there are countries that have chosen to close their borders. The most painful thing is that to take such a decision they had to close their hearts. And our missionary work must also reach those hearts that are closed to the reception of others.

'I do not know what else to say on this subject, except that it is a serious issue. Tonight we will have dinner. Many of these refugees have a piece of bread for dinner. Maybe we will have a cake. This brings back to me an image of Lesbos. I was there with Patriarch Bartholomew and the Orthodox archbishop of Athens, Ieronymos. They were all seated in rows, very neat – there were many thousands – and I was walking in front; behind me came Patriarch Bartholomew, and then Archbishop Ieronymos. I was saying goodbye, and at a certain moment I realized that the children were holding my hand but looking back. I asked myself: "What's up?" I turned around and saw that Patriarch Bartholomew had pockets full of sweets and was giving them to the children. With one hand they greeted me, with the other they grabbed the sweets. I thought maybe it was the only sweet thing they had eaten for days.

'And there is another image from Lesbos that helped me to cry a lot before God: a man of about 30 with three little children told me: "I am a Muslim. My wife was a Christian. We loved each other very much. The terrorists came one day. They saw her cross. They told her to take it off. She said no and they slit her throat before my very eyes. I continue to love my wife and my children."

'These things must be seen and must be told. These things do not come to the living rooms of our big cities. We are obliged to report and make public these human tragedies that some try to silence.'

'Many Jesuits here are involved in information, and as trainers we try to understand better what the Jesuit figure is today. You are a good Jesuit, committed to the mission entrusted to you. What can you tell us about that? What is your advice to young Jesuits in Myanmar on how to become a good Jesuit?'

'Don't teach them to be like me! [*Here the Pope burst out laughing.*] I will say two things. Among my teachers there was an elderly Jesuit who had been at the existential frontiers. He was a great Jesuit scientist, and he once gave me some advice: if you want to persevere in the Society, think clearly and speak obscurely. He was a great scientist, but he was a bad teacher. Do you understand? [*And here he laughed together with the other Jesuits.*] The second thing I want to mention concerns another man, and I want to mention him here in Myanmar, because I believe he never imagined that his name would be pronounced here. He was an Argentine Jesuit, and his name was

Miguel Angel Fiorito. He made a critical edition of the *Memoriale* by St Peter Favre, but he was a philosopher and had written his thesis on St Thomas and the natural human desire to find God. He was a professor of philosophy, dean of the Faculty, but he loved spirituality. And he taught us students the spirituality of St Ignatius. It was he who taught us the path of discernment. You who are a teacher, if you meet a Jesuit who is doing his training but cannot discern, who has not learned discernment and who shows little intention of learning it, even if he is an excellent young man, tell him to look for another path. The Jesuit must be a master of discernment, for himself and for others. St Ignatius did not ask us to do two examinations of conscience a day to get rid of lice or fleas. No, he did it because we would like to see what happens in our heart. In my opinion, the vocational criterion for the Society is this: can the candidate discern? Will he learn to discern? If he knows how to discern, he knows how to recognize what comes from God and what comes from the bad spirit, and this is enough for him to go on. Even if he does not understand much, even if they fail him at the exams … it is OK, as long as he knows spiritual discernment. Think of St Peter Claver. He knew how to discern and knew that God wanted him to spend his life among the black slaves. Meanwhile some esteemed theologians were discussing whether or not they had a soul.'

'My training lasted 14 years from novitiate to priestly ordination. Along the way other companions in formation left. We local Jesuit priests are now only three. What are your words of encouragement for those in formation?'

'One of the things the Lord respects is liberty, including the liberty to get away from Him, the freedom to sin. He is silent and suffers. He doesn't say anything. This is the extreme. Between that extreme and here, there are many situations that are not a sin, but are historical situations that weaken the person or make it clear that this was not his path ... The abandonment of the religious life, the abandonment of a priest, is a mystery. And we must respect him, help him if he asks for help, remain available and pray for him. In fact, the Lord awaits him at the most opportune moment. And we must never despair, because the Lord is good and even cunning, if you will pardon the word.

'I would like to add something about God's cunning: I want to tell you about a work of art that strikes me. It is a chapel located in the church of St Mary Magdalene in Vézelay, in the centre of France, where the Way of St James begins. On one side of the chapel there is Judas hanged, with his tongue out, his eyes open, dead. And next to him the devil is ready to take him away. On the other side of the chapel is the figure of the Good Shepherd, who has grabbed him, put him on his shoulders and taken him away. That

13th-century sculptor was an artist, but in his heart he was also a theologian. He was a mystic. And he was brave. He took leave to say something that none of us, no theologian, would dare to say officially: God is clever. God is cunning. And he is special. If we look carefully at the Good Shepherd's lips, we see that he wears a joking smile as if he were saying to the devil: "I fooled you."

'This teaches me a lot. Always to hope … it is the same sentence that the Curé d'Ars told the widow of someone who committed suicide, anguished because her husband had gone to hell: "Madam, between the bridge from which your husband threw himself and the river there is the mercy of God." Never forget the word mercy.'

'I am a Jesuit in formation as a teacher and I work in a slum as a teacher. People are very poor, but people there want to help each other. A girl asked me: "How can I help those in need if I need help myself?" I tried to give her an intellectual answer, but it did not convince me. Then someone advised me to ask the Holy Father the question.'

'Intellectual answers don't help. I am not an anti-intellectual, let's be clear! We need to study a lot, but an intellectual and abstract response in this case does not help. For a mother who has lost her son, for a man who has lost his wife, a child, a sick man … what can words do? Just a look … a smile, shaking hands, arms, touch … and perhaps at that point the Lord will inspire a word in us. But do not give explanations. And the question the girl asked was an existential question: "How can I, who have nothing, help others?" Come closer! And think about how that person can help you. Come closer. Accompany. Stay close. And the Holy Spirit – let us not forget that we have the Spirit inside – will inspire in you what you can do, what you can say. Because to speak is the last thing. First, do. Be silent, accompany, stay close. Proximity, nearness. It is the mystery of the Word made flesh. Nearness. Maybe you can tell the girl, "Be closer!" She needs closeness. And you need closeness too. And let God do the rest.'

'Holy Father, I wonder why you always find time to visit the Jesuits during your travels. And another question: what are the three important things that a Jesuit can do for the people of this country, for the Church in Myanmar?'

'The reason why I always meet the Jesuits is so as not to forget that I am a missionary and that I must convert sinners! [*The Pope thus provoked those present to laughter.*] As for the question, I like your use of the word "Church". Ignatius cared deeply for feeling with the Church, for feeling in the Church. And this also requires discernment. But we must be close to the hierarchy. And if I do not agree with what the bishop says, I must have the *parresia* to go and talk to him with courage and dialogue. And eventually obey.

Remember St Ignatius when Gian Pietro Carafa, Pope Paul IV, was elected. When he was asked what would happen to him if the Pope were to dissolve the Society, I believe St Ignatius replied that with a little prayer he would have fixed everything. And he would have remained in peace. But one cannot think of the Society of Jesus as a parallel Church, or a sub-Church. We all belong to the holy and sinful Church. We belong to the Church in joy and sadness. We have examples of great Jesuits who felt crucified by the Church of their time and kept their mouths shut. Let's think of Cardinal De Lubac, to name one. And many others. I would say: be men of the Church. When the Society gets into the orbit of self-sufficiency, it stops being the Society of Jesus.'

'A serious problem here is fundamentalism. I come from a region where there are many tensions with Muslims. I wonder how you can take care of people who have this tendency toward fundamentalism. What do you feel about this, visiting our country?'

'Look, there are fundamentalisms everywhere. And we Catholics have "the honour" of having fundamentalists among the baptized. I think it would be interesting if some of you who are preparing for graduation were to study the roots of fundamentalism. It is an attitude of the soul that stands as a judge of others and of those who share their religion. It is a going to the essential – a claim to be going to the essential – of religion, but to such an extent as to forget what is existential. It forgets the consequences. Fundamentalist attitudes take different forms, but they have the common background of underlining the essential so much that they deny the existential. The fundamentalist denies history, denies the person. And Christian fundamentalism denies the Incarnation.'

The meeting concluded in a festive atmosphere with the 'Salve Regina' and then with personal greetings and photographs.

On the afternoon of 1 December 2017, during his visit to Bangladesh, the Pope attended an ecumenical and inter-religious meeting for peace together with four religious representatives (a Muslim, a Hindu, a Buddhist and a Catholic) and a representative of civil society. The final prayer was recited by an Anglican bishop. Then a group of Rohingya came up onto the stage. The Pope welcomed them, listened to their stories and asked one of them to pray. At the end he went to the Apostolic Nunciature of Dhaka, where 13 Jesuits who carry out their mission in that country were waiting for him in a room, seated in a circle.

The superior of the mission expressed the joy of the Jesuits at having the Pope there with them: 'We are a group of Jesuits working in Bangladesh. Nine of us are from here, three from India and one from Belgium. God has blessed us, and we work here in Bangladesh in three dioceses. The mission has another 14 scholastics, three juniors and three novices. We work in a house for spiritual exercises and in formation, in parish ministries, in the educational apostolate and in the service of refugees. The first presence of the Jesuits in this land dates back to the end of the 16th century. In 1600 a church was built, but the following year it was destroyed. After various events we have been back in Bangladesh since 1994, when we were invited by the local Church. Today you give us the privilege of meeting you. We all feel proud to be Jesuits and we ask for your blessing. Today, I had considered giving a speech, but then I thought better of it: better to have an open conversation.'

The Pope replied to the greeting by saying: 'The two dates you mentioned have attracted my attention: 1600 and 1994. So for centuries the Jesuits have lived alternating vicissitudes without a stable presence. And that's OK: the Jesuits live like that too. Fr Hugo Rahner said that a Jesuit must be a man who is capable of moving while practising discernment, both in the field of God and in the field of the devil. Your years have been a little like this: a move without stability and a move forward in the light of discernment.'

'Holy Father, thank you for talking about the Rohingya people. They are our brothers and sisters, and you spoke of them in these terms: as brothers and sisters. Our Provincial sent two of us to help them.'

'Jesus Christ today is called Rohingya. You talk about them as brothers and sisters: They are. I think of St Peter Claver, who is very dear to me. He worked with the slaves of his time ... and to think that some theologians of the time – not so many, thank God – discussed whether the slaves had a soul or not! His life was a prophecy, and he helped his brothers and sisters who lived in shameful conditions. But this shame today is not over. Today there is much discussion about how to save the banks. The problem is the salvation of the banks. But who saves the dignity of men and women today? Nobody cares about people in ruins any longer. The devil manages to do this in today's world. If we had a little sense of reality, this should scandalize us. The media scandal today concerns the banks and not the people. In front of all this we must ask for a grace: to cry. The world has lost the gift of tears. St Ignatius – who had this experience – asked for the gift of tears. St Peter Fabre did so too. Once we used to ask for the gift of tears during Mass. The prayer was: "Lord, you made water flow from the rock; make tears flow from my sinful heart." The impudence of our world is such that the only solution is to pray and ask for the grace of tears. But this evening, in front of those poor people I met, I felt ashamed! I felt ashamed of myself, for the whole world! Sorry, I'm just trying to share my feelings with you.'

'How can the Society of Jesus respond today to the needs of Bangladesh?'

'Honestly, I know little about the activities of the Society of Jesus in Bangladesh. But the fact that the Provincial charged two Jesuits with the responsibility to work in the refugee camps makes me understand that the Jesuits are on the move! And this is precisely our vocation, and it is well said in one word of the "Formula of the Institute of the Society": *discurrir*, that is ... move forward, move ... get about ... try the spirits ... This is beautiful and it is right for our vocation.'

'We feel blessed that you came to Bangladesh, a nation where there is such a small Christian community. And you made the archbishop of our capital a cardinal. Why such attention to us?'

'I have to say that Bangladesh was a surprise for me too: there's so much wealth! Naming the cardinals, I tried to look at small Churches, those that grow in the peripheries, at the edges. Not to give consolation to those Churches, but to launch a clear message: the small Churches that grow in the periphery and are without ancient Catholic traditions today must speak to the universal Church, to the whole Church. I clearly feel that they have something to teach us.'

'How do you feel today after celebrating Mass with Catholics? Did you manage to greet children as you usually do?'

'Yes. I greeted some of them. And tonight I greeted the two Rohingya girls. Children give me tenderness. Tenderness is good in this cruel world: we need it. I want to add something about it: St Ignatius was mystical. His true figure has been rediscovered recently. We had a rigid image of him. But he was a mother to the sick people! He was capable of a deep tenderness, which he manifested on many occasions. It was Fr Arrupe who, as General of the Society, repeated these things to us and showed us Ignatius' profound soul. He founded the Ignatian Spirituality Center and the *Christus* magazine to refine our spirituality further. For me, he is a prophetic figure. Your question makes me think of how important it is to have a heart capable of tenderness and compassion for those who are weak or poor or small.

'And remember that it was Fr Arrupe who founded the Jesuit Refugee Service. In Bangkok, before taking the plane on which he had a stroke, he said: "Pray, pray, pray." This was the sense of the discourse that he addressed there to the Jesuits who are working with the refugees: not to neglect prayer. This was his valediction. This was precisely his last legacy left to the Society. Do you understand? Sociology is important, yes, but prayer matters more, much more.'

Our thoughts went immediately to the fact that shortly before, in his meeting with the Rohingya, the Pope had concluded not with a sociological discourse but by asking one of them to raise a prayer, and to pray together. At this point the Pope asked if there were any further questions, but one of them replied: 'No. Your presence here among us is more than many answers!' The encounter ended with the blessing of rosaries and some group photos.

In meditating on the words used by the Pontiff in these conversations it is always necessary to remember what he himself wrote in the preface to a volume that contains, *inter alia*, his earlier conversations with Jesuits during his trips: 'I must say that I felt these moments as being very free, especially when they happen during my journeys: this is the occasion to make my first thoughts on that trip. I feel at home I speak our family's language, and I do not fear misunderstandings. So what I say can sometimes be a little risky.' And he added: 'Sometimes what I feel I have to say, I say to myself; it is important for me too. In the conversations some important things are born in me, upon which I can then reflect.'[2]

10

WHERE HAVE OUR PEOPLE BEEN CREATIVE? JESUITS IN CHILE AND PERU

On Tuesday, 16 January 2018, at 7 p.m., on his first full day of an apostolic journey to Chile and Peru, Pope Francis met with 90 Chilean Jesuits in the Centro Hurtado of Santiago. On arrival he was shown a reproduction of the green Ford van that St Alberto Hurtado had used to bring aid to the city's marginalized: it is a true symbol of apostolic passion. The Pope was accompanied by the Provincial, Fr Cristián del Campo, into the chapel where the remains of the Jesuit saint are kept. Inaugurated in 1995, the sanctuary houses the tomb of the saint, a stone sarcophagus containing clumps of earth from each region of Chile, which together symbolize the embrace of the country's faithful. The Provincial greeted the Pope in the name of all the Jesuits – including, notably, many young ones – and asked him: 'How are things going in Chile, and have you felt welcome in our country?' The meeting quickly became warm and familial. Fr Del Campo presented two of those present, Frs Carlos and José Aldunate, blood brothers, aged 101 and 100 years respectively.

Antonio Spadaro SJ

Francis began with these words:

'I am so pleased to see Fr Carlos! He was my spiritual director in 1960 for my juniorate. José was the master of novices, and then they made him Provincial. Carlos was the caretaker and was ... the king of common sense! He could give spiritual advice with really good sense. I recall one time I went to him because I was very angry with someone. I wanted to face up to that person and tell him off. Carlos advised me: "Calm down! Do you really want to fall out with him immediately? Try other ways ..." I have never forgotten that advice, and I thank him for it now. Yes, in Chile I immediately felt very welcome. I arrived yesterday. Today I have been very well received. I have seen many gestures of dear affection. Now, ask me whatever you want.'

A Jesuit stepped forward: 'I would like to ask what have been the great joys and disappointments that you have experienced during your pontificate.'

'This time of the pontificate is a quite peaceful time. As soon as I realized during the conclave what was about to happen – a complete surprise for me – I felt great peace. And up to today that peace has never left me. It is a gift of the Lord, and I am grateful for it.

And I really hope he won't take it away from me. It is a peace that I feel as a pure gift, a pure gift. There is something that does not take peace away from me, but which does hurt me, and that is gossip. I don't like gossip; it makes me sad. It often spreads in closed-off worlds. When it happens in a world of priests and religious, I want to ask: how is this possible? You left everything, you decided not to have a wife alongside you, you didn't marry, you had no children ... Do you want to finish as a gossiping old bachelor? Oh, my God, what a sad life!'

A Jesuit from the Argentine-Uruguayan province asked: 'What resistance have you encountered during your pontificate, and how have you faced it? Have you made discernment?'

'I never call a difficulty a "resistance", because to do so would be to renounce discernment. I prefer to discern. It is easy to say there is resistance and not realize that a moment of conflict is actually bringing out some crumbs of truth. So I think that such conflicts can help me. I often ask a person: "What do you think?" This would help me to relativize many things that at first sight might seem like resistances but which are actually a reaction that comes from a misunderstanding, from the fact that some things need to be repeated, better explained ... This might be a weakness of mine, the fact that sometimes I take things for granted and make a logical jump without explaining the process clearly, for I am convinced that the person I am talking to has quickly grasped my reasoning. I am aware that, if I go back and explain things better, then at that point the other person will say, "Ah, yes, agreed." All in all, it is very helpful for me to examine the meaning of conflicts carefully. But when I am aware that there is true resistance, certainly, I am displeased. Some say to me that it is normal that there is resistance when someone wants to make changes. The famous "this has always been done this way" reigns everywhere: "It has always been done this way, why should we change? If things are the way they are, they have always been done this way, so why change?" This is a great temptation that we all faced in the period after the Second Vatican Council. The resistances are still present and try to tell us to relativize the Council, to water it down. I am even sadder when someone joins a campaign of resistance. And alas, I see this too. You asked me about resistances, and I cannot deny that there are some, then. I see them and I know them.

'There are doctrinal resistances that you know about better than I. For my own good I do not read the content of internet sites of this so-called "resistance". I know who they are, I know the groups, but I do not read them for my own mental health. If there is something very serious, they tell me about it so that I know. You know them … It is displeasing, but you have to go on. Historians tell us that it takes a century for a Council to put down its roots. We are halfway there.

'Sometimes we ask: but that man, that woman, have they read the Council? And there are people who have not read the Council. And if they have read it, they have not understood it. Fifty years on! We studied philosophy before the Council, but we had the advantage of studying theology after it. We lived through the change of perspective, and the Council documents were already there.

'When I perceive resistance, I seek dialogue whenever it is possible; but some resistance comes from people who believe they possess the true doctrine and accuse you of being a heretic. When I cannot see spiritual goodness in what these people say or write, I simply pray for them. I find it sad, but I won't settle on this sentiment for the sake of my own mental well-being.'

Then came a question from a novice: 'Many people identify the Church with the bishops and priests. And they are very critical of them for the way they live out their poverty, for the restrictions on the participation of women and limited space given to minorities. Faced with this opinion, what would you propose in order to bring the Church hierarchy, of which we are a part, closer to the people?'

'I have just said to the bishops what I think of the relationship between the bishop and the people of

God. And so, what I think about bishops you will find in that talk. It was short, for we had two long meetings last year during their *ad limina* visits. Clericalism is the most serious damage endured by the Church in Latin America today: that is, the failure to be aware that the Church is the entire holy and faithful people of God, who are infallible *in credendo*, all together. I speak of Latin America for I know it best.

'Some time ago I wrote a letter to the Pontifical Commission for Latin America, and today I come back to the theme. We need to be aware that the grace of being a missionary comes from baptism, not from sacred orders or religious vows.

'It is a consolation to see many priests and religious men and women putting their entire lives at stake: that is, with the conciliar option of placing themselves at the service of the people of God. But some still behave like princes. The people of God must be given their own space.

'And the same can be said about the theme of women. I had a special experience when I was a diocesan bishop: we needed to look at a specific theme, and a consultation process began – obviously just between priests and bishops – and we had completed our reflection that led us to a number of questions on which a decision needed to be taken. But the same issue, treated during a combined meeting of men and women, led to much richer conclusions, much more practical, much more fruitful. It is that simple experience that comes to mind now, but it makes me reflect. Women need to give the Church all the richness that von Balthasar called "the Marian dimension". Without this dimension the Church limps or uses crutches, and so walks badly. And I believe that the road is long … And I repeat, as I said today to the bishops: "un-princify", be near to the people.'

Fr Juan Díaz spoke up and the Pope recognized him. 'Juanito!'

After a warm personal greeting, Fr Díaz continued: 'Francis, on different occasions and in *Evangelii gaudium* you have warned about the dangers of worldliness. Which aspects of our life should we Jesuits be careful about so as not to fall into the temptation of worldliness?'

'The warning about worldliness came to me from the final chapter of the *Meditations on the Church*, by Henri de Lubac. He quotes a Benedictine, Dom Anscar Vonier, who speaks of worldliness as the worst evil that can befall the Church. This stirred in me the desire to understand worldliness better. Certainly, St Ignatius wrote about it in his *Spiritual Exercises,* in the third exercise of the first week, where he asks us to discover the deceits of the world. The three graces we ask for in that meditation are repentance of sins – that is, the pain of sins – shame and the awareness of the world, from the devil and his things. So, in our spirituality, worldliness should be remembered and considered as a temptation.

'It would be superficial to state that worldliness is just leading a life that is relaxed and frivolous. These are just consequences. Worldliness is the use of criteria of the world and following the criteria of the world and choosing to use the criteria of the world. It means making a discernment and preferring the criteria of the world. So what we must be asking ourselves is what are these criteria of the world. And this is precisely what St Ignatius makes us ask in this third exercise. He has us make three supplications: to the Father, to the Lord and to the Virgin. May they help us discover these criteria! Each of us then must set about discovering what is worldly in our own lives. A simple and general response will not suffice. In what way am I worldly? This is the true question. It is not enough to say what worldliness is in general. For example, a theology professor can become worldly if he goes in search of the latest thoughts so as to be fashionable: this is worldliness. And there can be a thousand other examples. We should ask the Lord not to be deceived in seeking to discern what is our own worldliness.'

Another question followed: 'Holy Father, you have always been a man of reforms. Besides those of the Curia and the Church, in which reforms can we Jesuits support you the most?'

'I think that one of the things that the Church is in most need of today is discernment. This is put very clearly in the pastoral perspectives and objectives of *Amoris laetitia*. We are used to a "yes you can or no you can't" mentality. The morality used in *Amoris laetitia* is the more classic Thomist one – that is, the one from St Thomas himself, not the decadent version of later Thomism that some have studied. I too received a formation in the way of thinking of "Yes you can or no you can't", or "Up to this point you can, up to here you can't". I wonder if you remember [*and here the Pope looked at one of those present*] that Colombian Jesuit who came to teach morals at the Collegio Massimo? When he was teaching the sixth commandment, someone dared to ask: "Can a man and a woman who are engaged to be married kiss each other?" If they could kiss each other! Do you get it? And he replied: "Yes they can! No problem! They just have to put a tissue between them." This is a *forma mentis* (a way of thinking) for doing theology generally. It is a *forma mentis* that is based on a limit. And we bear the consequences.

'If you take a look at the panorama of reactions to *Amoris laetitia*, you will see that the strongest criticisms of the exhortation are against the eighth chapter: "Can a divorced person receive communion, or not?" But *Amoris laetitia* goes in a completely different direction; it does not enter into these distinctions. It raises the issue of discernment. This was already at the heart of truly great classic Thomist morality. So the contribution that I want from the Society is to help the Church to grow in discernment. Today the Church needs to grow in discernment. And to us the Lord has given this family grace to discern. I do not know if you know this, but I have said it during other similar meetings with Jesuits: at the end of Fr Ledóchowski's time as Superior General, the highest work of the spirituality of the Society was the *Epitome*. Everything you had to do was all regulated in an enormous mix of the *Formula of the Institution*, the *Constitutions* and the rules. There were even rules for the cook. And it was all mixed, without following a hierarchy. Fr Ledóchowski was a great friend of the Abbot General of the Benedictines, and once he went to visit him bringing along this volume. Shortly after, the abbot sought him out and said: "Father General, with this you have killed the Society of Jesus." And he was right, for the *Epitome* took away any room for discernment.

'Then came the Second World War. Fr Janssens had to guide the Society after the war, and he did it as well as he could, for it was not easy. And then came the grace of the Generalate of Fr Pedro Arrupe with his Ignatian Spirituality Center, the journal *Christus* and the impulse given to the *Spiritual Exercises*. He renewed this family grace of discernment. He overcame the *Epitome*; he went back to the lesson of the

fathers, to Favre and Ignatius. Here we should recognize the role of the life of the *Christus* journal for
that period. And then also the role of Fr Luis González
with his centre of spirituality: he went around to the
entire Society to give the *Spiritual Exercises*. He went
about opening doors, refreshing this aspect that today
we see has grown greatly in the Society. I would say,
recalling this family history, that there was a moment
when we had lost – or I do not know if we had lost
it, let's say we did not use it much – the sense of discernment. Today, give it – let's give it! – to the Church,
which is crying out for it.'

The last question was from a theologian from the
province of Peru: 'A question on collaboration: what
help has the Society been giving to you during your
pontificate? How has there been collaboration? What
relationship do you have with the Society?'

'Since the second day after the election! Fr Adolfo
Nicolás came into my room at Casa Santa Marta ...
That's how the collaboration began. He came to greet
me. I was still living in the small room that I had been
given for the conclave, not the one I have now, and
we conversed there. And the Superiors General, both
Adolfo and now Arturo, have concentrated much on
this. I think that on this point ... Fr Spadaro is here.'

Spadaro: 'I'm here!'

'There he is, in the gallery ... I think he has been
the witness of this relationship with the Society since

175

the first moment. The availability is total. And with intelligence too, as for example on the doctrine of the faith: there has been great support. But nobody could accuse the current pontificate of "Jesuitism". I say it and I believe I am being sincere in saying so. It is a matter of ecclesial collaboration, in the ecclesial spirit. It is a (*sentire*) listening and feeling with the Church and in the Church, respecting the charism of the Society. And the documents of the last General Congregation did not need pontifical approval. I have not thought it necessary at all, for the Society is an adult. And if it makes a mistake … complaints will arrive and then we'll see. I think this is the way we collaborate.

'All right, thank you very much … but I want to say one more very important thing to you, a recommendation: the account of conscience! For Jesuits this is a gem, a family grace … Please, don't overlook it!'

The private meeting naturally spilled over into the open space of the sanctuary. A group of people had gathered there who have benefited from the solidarity programmes run by the Church: representatives of workers, students, the elderly, the homeless and migrants. In his greeting, Jesuit Fr Pablo Walker, the chaplain general of Hogar de Cristo, said, 'Dear Pope Francis, the table is ready and we give you a warm welcome. Years ago we invited you to come and drink with us, and now that day has arrived.'

Recalling that 'to eat is a miracle', the chaplain asked the Pope to bless the *sopaipillas* that had been prepared by Mrs Sonia Castro and her daughter Isabella Reinal. The Pope pronounced the prayer of blessing: 'May the Lord bless this food that we are sharing, which has been made by you; may He bless the hands that made it, the hands that distribute it and the hands that receive it. May the Lord bless the hearts of all of us, and may this sharing teach us also to share the way, to share life and then to share paradise. Amen.' After receiving the Bible of the People of God as a gift and having offered a painting of Jesus the Merciful by Terezia Sedlakova as a gift to the Sanctuary, the Pope recited the Lord's Prayer with all the participants. Then he imparted his blessing.

———

At the end of his first complete day in Peru, 19 January 2018, and after making a courtesy visit to President Pedro Pablo Kuczynski, the Pope went to the Jesuit church of St Peter. The Society of Jesus started building it in the 16th century, and it is now considered one of the most important religious complexes in the historical centre of Lima. It is also the national sanctuary of the Sacred Heart of Jesus. Its layout echoes that of the church of Il Gesù in Rome. The façade is in a neoclassical style and there are three entry doors.

There is a dominating neo-classical bell-tower. Inside the furnishings are in a rich Baroque style that is well lit by sunlight. Off the three naves lie ten chapels. St Peter's is considered one of the most beautiful churches in Peru.

At the entrance to the penitentiary chapel Francis was welcomed by the Provincial, Fr Juan Carlos Morante, and by the local superior, Fr José Enrique Rodríguez. Crossing the left nave of the church, the Pope reached the sacristy, where about a hundred Jesuits were gathered. Fr Morante thanked Francis for his visit and spoke of the work of the Society in the evangelization of indigenous peoples in the field of education, remembering Frs Alonso de Barzana (1528–1598), Francisco del Castillo (1615–1673), Antonio Ruiz de Montoya (1585–1652) and others. He spoke of the new perspectives from the Second Vatican Council and of the new challenges: the preferential option for the poor, the *Spiritual Exercises*, the collaboration with the laity and the new apostolic challenges, which require a new apostolic discernment. Then the Pope spoke. The text of the conversation transcribed here has been approved for publication in this form by the Pontiff.

Francis greeted those present in this way:

'Good evening. ... Thank you. Let's begin to converse without wasting time. You've prepared some questions ... ask away.'

The first question was: 'We Peruvian Jesuits have always been engaged with the themes of reconciliation and justice, especially in recent years. Now it seems that the political forces have suddenly reached an agreement, and reconciliation seems to be an appeal for all. Reconciliation is being proposed without there having been a process. My question is: what stance should we take, what should we bear in mind when we want reconciliation? We feel that the word "reconciliation" is being manipulated and we feel that justice is being proposed that has not been sufficiently elaborated. What are your thoughts?'

'Thank you. The word "reconciliation" is not only being manipulated, it is being ruined. Today – not just here, for this applies in other Latin American countries too – the word "reconciliation" has been emptied of its power. When St Paul describes the reconciliation of all with God, in Christ, he delivers a strong word. Today, however, "reconciliation" has become wrapping paper. It's been emptied out. It's been weakened not only of its religious content but also of its human content, that is, what we share when we look each other in the eye. Instead, today, it is being done under the counter.

'I would say that these stunts should not be accepted, nor should we struggle against them. We must say to those who adopt it in its weaker form: use it, but we won't use it, for the concept has been demolished. We do need to continue to work, however, seeking to reconcile people. From below, from the sides, with a good word, with a visit, with a course to help understanding, with the weapon of prayer that will give us strength and make miracles, but especially with the human weapon of persuasion, which is humility. Persuasion acts through humility.

'I propose this path: go and find the adversary, put yourselves before them, if there is the opportunity … persuasion! Considering the reconciliation that is being proposed today, I don't want to speak about the detail of what is happening in Peru because I don't know the situation, but I do trust your words, and given that, as I said, this is happening in other Latin American countries, I could say to you that this is not so much a true and profound reconciliation as a negotiation. OK, the art of political leadership implies knowing how to negotiate. The issue is what can be negotiated in an agreement. If among the pile of things you bring to the negotiating table there is stuff regarding your own private interests, then it won't work … We are not talking about an agreement. This is something else.

'So, instead of "reconciliation" it is better to speak of "hope". Seek out a word that is not a short-sighted pet project, being used without its full meaning. I want to repeat this: I am not an expert on the details of the situation in Peru, I trust your words, but it is a phenomenon across Latin American countries; this is why I can say what I say.'

This question followed: 'Holy Father, our province is losing numbers, people are getting old, young people are taking on new responsibilities ... We still have many institutions. The situation is not very easy. How can you encourage us, how can you invite us to continue to strengthen our vocation to follow Jesus, to live in the Society of Jesus in these circumstances, which can sometimes seem to be discouraging? How can we not become bitter and resentful, but instead seek to live these circumstances joyfully? What should we say to those who are growing old and see behind them fewer people, who won't be able to continue what was done in the past with the same strength? What should we say to the youngest today, who find difficult situations all around them?'

'You said that we have many "institutions". Let me correct a word: we have many "works". We need to distinguish between works and institutions. The institutional aspect of the Society is essential. But not all the works are institutions. Perhaps they were, but time has ensured that they stopped being institutions. We need to discern between what today is an institution – that attracts, gives you strength, that is prophetic – and what instead is a work that, yes, has been an institution in its time, but seems now to have stopped being so. And what has always been done must be done again: a pastoral and community discernment.

'Fr Arrupe insisted on this. We need to choose the works with this criterion: that they are institutions, in the Ignatian sense of the word – that is to say, they attract people and respond to the needs of today. And this demands a community that places itself in a state of discernment. And perhaps this is your challenge ... Considering this decrease of young people and energy, institutional desolation can take over. No, don't allow it! The Society went through a period of institutional desolation during the Generalate of Fr Ricci, who ended up a prisoner in Castel Sant'Angelo.[1] The letters that Fr Ricci wrote to the Society in that period are a marvel of criteria of discernment, criteria of action to not allow ourselves be dragged down by institutional desolation. Desolation pulls you down, it is a wet blanket they throw at you to see how you cope, bringing you to bitterness, to disillusionment. This is the post-triumphalist discourse of Emmaus: "We had hoped ..." We do this ourselves, for example, when we use expressions like "the glorious Society was something else", "the light cavalry of the Church ... but now ..." and so on.

'The spirit of desolation leaves deep marks. I advise you to read the letters of Fr Ricci. Later, Fr Roothaan went through another period of desolation for the Society due to the Freemasons, but it was not as strong as that of Fr Ricci, which culminated in the suppression.[2] And there have been other periods like it in the history of the Society.

'On the other hand, we need to look to the fathers, the fathers of the institutionalization of the Society: obviously Ignatius and Faber ... Here we can speak of Fr Barzana.[3] I am fascinated by the figure of Barzana, who spoke 12 indigenous languages when he was at Santiago del Estero in Argentina. They called him "the Francis Xavier of the West". And there that man planted the seed of faith in the desert, he established the faith. They say he was of Jewish origin, and that his name was Bar Shana. It is good to look to these men who were able to institutionalize and didn't let themselves become discouraged. I ask if Xavier was desolate in his failure to see China without being able to enter. No. I imagine that he turned to the Lord, saying: "You do not want it, so goodbye, that's OK." He followed the road that was proposed to him, and in this case it was death! ... but that's OK!

'Desolation: we should not let this become part of our lives. Instead we should seek out the Jesuits who are consoled. I don't know. I don't want to give advice, but ... always seek consolation. Seek it always. As a touchstone for your own spiritual lives.

'As with Xavier on the border of China, always look forward ... God knows! But the smile of the heart should not be left to wither. I don't know. I can't give you any recipes. In a climate of consolation what is needed is discernment of the ministries and the institutional aspect. So read the letters of Fr Lorenzo Ricci. It is marvellous how he wanted to choose consolation at the moment of the greatest desolation that the Society has ever known, when he knew that the European courts were about to give the Society its *coup de grâce*.'

'I would like you to say something about a theme that leads to a lot of desolation in the Church, and particularly among religious men and women and the clergy: the theme of sexual abuse. We are very disturbed by these scandals. What can you say to us about them? A word of encouragement ...'

'Yesterday I spoke to the priests and religious men and women of Chile in the cathedral of Santiago. This is the greatest desolation that the Church is suffering. It brings shame, but we need to remember that shame is also a very Ignatian grace, a grace that St Ignatius asks us to make in the three colloquies of the first week. And so let us take it as a grace and be fully ashamed. We have to love the Church with her wounds. Many wounds ...

'Let me tell you something. On 24 March Argentina remembers the military coup d'état, the dictatorship, the *desaparecidos* [the disappeared] ... and every 24 March the Plaza de Mayo fills to remember it. One year, on 24 March, I left the archbishop's house and went to serve as confessor for the Carmelite sisters. On my return I took the subway and got out six blocks away from the Plaza de Mayo. The Plaza was full … and I walked those six blocks to enter by the side. When I was about to cross a road, there was a couple with a child about two or three years old, and the child was running ahead. The father said to him: "Come, come, come here … Be careful of the paedophiles!" How shameful I felt! What shame! They didn't realize that I was the archbishop, I was a priest and … what shame!

'Occasionally someone might even say: "OK. Look at the statistics … I don't know … 70 per cent of paedophiles are in the family setting, people known to the family. Then at the gyms and in the swimming pools. The percentage of paedophiles who are Catholic priests does not reach 2 per cent, it's 1.6 per cent. It is not that much." But it is terrible even if only one of our brothers is such! For God anointed him to sanctify children and adults, and instead of making them holy he has destroyed them. It's horrible! We need to listen to what someone who has been abused feels. On Fridays – sometimes this is known and sometimes it is not known – I normally meet some of them. In Chile I also had such a meeting. As their experience is very hard, they remain annihilated. Annihilated!

'For the Church this is a great humiliation. It shows not only our fragility but also, let us say so clearly, our level of hypocrisy. In cases of corruption, in the sense of abuse of an institutional type, it is notable that there are some newer Congregations whose founders have fallen into these abuses. These cases are public. Pope Benedict had to suppress a large male Congregation. The founder had spread such habits. He abused young and immature religious men. It was a Congregation that had a female branch, and the female founder had also spread such habits. Benedict had started the process on the women's branch. I had to suppress it. You here have many painful cases. But it is curious that the phenomenon of abuse touched some new, prosperous Congregations.

'Abuse in these Congregations is always the fruit of a mentality tied to power that has to be healed in its malicious roots. And I will add: there are three levels of abuse that come together: abuse of authority (mixing the internal forum with the external), sexual abuse and an economic mess.

'There is always money involved. The devil enters through the wallet. Ignatius places the first step of the devil's temptations in riches ... then come vanity and pride, but first of all, it's riches. The three levels come together very often in the new Congregations that have fallen into this problem of abuse.

'Forgive my lack of humility in suggesting that you read what I said to the Chileans. That material is more carefully articulated and reasoned than what comes to me spontaneously now.'

'Help us in this process of discernment of the universal Society. Fr Sosa asks us to reflect on where the

Society should go today, considering our strengths and weaknesses. You have a universal vision, you know us well, you know what our contribution to the universal Church could be. You could help us by saying, for example, how you see that the Spirit is moving the Church today towards the future. In which direction should we be following the paths of the Spirit, as Jesuits, in the places we already are – and not just in the province of Peru – to be at the service of the Spirit? Some guidance that could partially transform our programme ...'

'Thank you. I'll reply with just one word. It might seem that I am saying nothing, but instead I am saying everything. And the word is "Council". Pick up again the Second Vatican Council, and read *Lumen gentium*. Yesterday, with the bishops of Chile – or was it the day before, I don't even know what day it is! – I encouraged them to declericalize. If there is something that is very clear, it is the awareness of the faithful holy people of God, infallible *in credendo,* as the Council teaches us. This brings the Church forward. The grace of being missionary and proclaiming Jesus Christ comes to us in baptism. From there we can move forward ...

'We should never forget that evangelization is done by the Church as a people of God. The Lord wants an evangelizing Church, I see that clearly. This came from my heart, in simplicity, in the few minutes I spoke during the general congregations before the conclave.

A Church that goes out, a Church that goes out proclaiming Jesus Christ. After or in that very moment when she adores and fills herself with him. I always use an example tied to the Book of Revelation, where we read: "I am at the door and knock. If someone opens I will enter" (cf. Rev. 3:20). The Lord is outside and wants to come in. Sometimes the Lord is inside and is knocking because he wants us to let him out! The Lord is asking us to be a Church outside, a Church that goes out. Church as a field hospital … Ah, the wounds of the people of God! Sometimes the people of God are wounded by a rigid, moralist catechism, of the "You can or you can't" variety, or by a lack of testimony.

'A poor Church for the poor! The poor are not a theoretical formula of the Communist Party. The poor are the heart of the Gospel. They are the centre of the Gospel. We cannot preach the Gospel without the poor. So I say to you: it is along these lines that I feel the Spirit is leading us. And there are strong resistances. But I must also say that for me the fact that resistances arise is a good sign. It is a sign that we are on the right road; this is the road. Otherwise the devil would not bother to resist.

'I would say these are the criteria: poverty, being missionaries, the conscience of the faithful people of God … In Latin America, particularly, you should ask: "But where have our people been creative?" With some deviations, yes, but it has been creative in its popular piety. And why have our people been able to be creative in popular piety? Because the clergy weren't interested, and so they let them do it ... the people went on ahead.

'And then, yes, what the Church is asking today of the Society – this I have said often, and Spadaro, who publishes these things, has grown tired of writing it – is to teach discernment with humility. Yes, as Pontiff, I ask this of you officially. Generally, above all, we who are part of the religious setting of life as priests and bishops often show little ability to discern, we don't know how to do it because we have been educated with a different theology, which is more formal. We go as far as "You can or you can't", as I said to the Chilean Jesuits concerning the resistance to *Amoris laetitia*. Some people are reducing the entire fruit of two Synods – all the work that has been done – to "You can or you can't". Help us to discern then. Certainly, someone who is not discerning cannot teach others to discern. And to be discerning you have to enter into practice, you have to examine yourself. You have to start with yourself.'

This was how the meeting concluded. The rector of the church then illustrated to the Pope the significance of the chair that had been prepared for him. In 1992 there was an attack by Sendero Luminoso, and a part of the church was damaged.[4] In the restoration work, the walls were strengthened and an architrave dating from 1672 was removed. It had been used to make the chair for this visit, and it was cut using Lima-style Baroque. The Pope thanked the rector, smiling, and made a joke: 'I sat on number 1672. I'll choose this number in the lottery!' At the end, the Provincial thanked the Pope before asking for a group photo. The Pope replied to the thanksgiving with these words:

'I thank you very much. Pray for me! I share with you a great grace: as soon as I realized that I was going to be elected Pope, I felt a great peace that has never yet abandoned me. Pray that the Lord will keep it for me!'

At the end of the encounter the Pope gave the Jesuits a silver cross made by the Italian goldsmith Antonio Vedele in 1981. It is inscribed with the Stations of the Cross. It portrays not 14 stations but 15. This is because the artist wanted to place between the two arms the representation of the resurrection of Christ. Vedele is the goldsmith who designed the pectoral cross used by Pope Francis. In 1998 it was cast in silver by his student Giuseppe Albrizzi, the artist of the crozier used by the then cardinal of Buenos Aires, Jorge Mario Bergoglio.

Finally, the Pope posed for a group photograph. Then he crossed the church of St Peter and, before going out the main door, he stopped before the tomb of the venerable Fr Francisco del Castillo, the apostle of Lima.

SOURCES

1. Wake up the World!
   'Svegliate il mondo!', *La Civiltà Cattolica*, 3925 (4 January 2014)

2. Go Out to the Peripheries of Existence
   Unedited account of the encounter on 16 January 2015 at the Apostolic Nunciature in Manila

3. A Shepherd's Footsteps
   Introductory interview with Pope Francis, *Nei tuoi occhi è la mia parola. Omelie e discorsi di Buenos Aires 1999–2013* (Rizzoli, Milan, 2016)

4. Not Everything in Life is Black and White
   'Oggi la Chiesa ha bisogno di crescere nel discernimento', *La Civiltà Cattolica*, 3989 (10 September 2016)

5. Distance Makes Us Ill
   'Intervista a Papa Francesco in occasione del viaggio apostolico in Svezia', *La Civiltà*

Cattolica, 3994 (26 November 2016); the text was also published in Swedish translation by *Dagens Nyheter*

6. Have Courage and Prophetic Daring
   'Avere coraggio e audacia profetica', *La Civiltà Cattolica*, 3995 (10 December 2016)

7. Take the Gospel without Tranquillizers
   'Il Vangelo va preso senza calmanti', *La Civiltà Cattolica*, 4000 (11–25 February 2017), partly pre-published in *Corriere della Sera* (9 February 2017)

8. Grace is Not an Ideology
   Pope Francis's private conversation with some Colombian Jesuits, *La Civiltà Cattolica* (28 September 2017)

9. At the Crossroads of History
   Conversations with the Jesuits in Myanmar and Bangladesh, *La Civiltà Cattolica* (14 December 2017)

10. 'Where Have Our People Been Creative?'
    Jesuits in Chile and Peru, *La Civiltà Cattolica* (15 February 2018)

NOTES

Chapter 1 Wake Up the World!

1 The Assembly was held between 17 and 29 November 2013 at the House of the Salesians in Rome. It was a meeting based on three experiences that guided subsequent reflections. Fr Janson Hervé, of the Little Brothers of Jesus, spoke of the 'lights that help me to live this service of my brothers and how Pope Francis comforts my hope'. Fr Mauro Jöhri, a Capuchin, explained 'how Pope Francis inspires me and challenges me at the service of the life of my Order'. Last of all, Fr Heinz Kulüke, of the Society of the Divine Word, dwelt on the 'leadership' within a religious missionary congregation in an international and intercultural context, in the light of Pope Francis's example.

2 Let us not forget that Jorge Mario Bergoglio, as a Provincial with the Argentinian Jesuits, had published *Meditaciones para religiosos* (San Miguel, Ediciones Diego de Torres, 1982), bringing together reflections delivered to his confrères, which prove illuminating when it comes to understanding some key terms that Bergoglio would subsequently go on to develop further. The volume was published in Italian translation: *Nel cuore di ogni padre* (Milan, Rizzoli, 2014).

3 Benedict XVI, homily at the inaugural Holy Mass of the 5th General Conference of the Episcopate of Latin America and the Caribbean in the Santuario de Aparecida (13 May 2007). Pope Francis returned to his predecessor's concept several times, for example in the homily at Casa San Marta on 1 October 2013, adding: 'When people and peoples see

this witness to humility, to mildness, to meekness, they feel the need of which the Prophet Zachariah speaks: "We want to come with you!" People feel this need in the face of witness to charity, to that humble charity, not self-important, which adores and serves.' We find the quotation from Benedict XVI in the speech given by Pope Francis on 4 October during his visit to the Cathedral of San Rufino in Assisi, and also in the apostolic exhortation *Evangeli gaudium* (no. 14).

4   Cf. Jorge Mario Bergoglio, *Nel cuore dell'uomo. Utopia e impegno* (Milan, Bompiani, 2013), pp. 23; Pope Francis, *La mia porta è sempre aperta* (Milan, Rizzoli, 2013), pp. 86ff. (*My Door is Always Open*, London, Bloomsbury, 2014).

5   Pope Francis expressed this conviction in his *Evangelii gaudium*, when he wrote: 'Our model is not the sphere, which is no greater than its parts, where every point is equidistant from the centre and there are no differences between one point and another. Instead it is the polyhedron, which reflects the convergence of all its parts, each of which preserves its distinctiveness' (no. 236).

6   Pope Francis is thinking of this letter by Fr Pedro Arrupe and had also quoted it in the interview with *La Civiltà Cattolica*, calling it 'brilliant'.

7   Cf. Pope Francis, *My Door is Always Open*.

8   The incomprehension was due to the fact that, in their missions, the Jesuits were trying to adapt the proclamation of the Gospel to local cultures and religions. But this had troubled some people, and voices had been raised against such attitudes, as if they involved a contamination of the Christian message. Prophetic positions were not accepted at the time, because they went beyond the ordinary understanding of events.

9   Fr Segundo Llorente (1906–1989), a Jesuit, spent over 40 years as a missionary in Alaska. He was elected to the

Legislature of the State of Alaska, which he is also credited with co-founding. He was buried in a cemetery in De Smet, Idaho, where only indigenous native Americans can be buried. When he arrived in Akularak, at the age of 29, his first difficulty consisted not only in learning Eskimo but also in speaking to God in person in a radically different way from the European. He wrote 12 books about his experience as a missionary.

10　Jorge Mario Bergoglio, speech at the encounter with the bishops at the Episcopal Latin American Council (CELAM) at the meeting of the Co-Ordinating Committee held at the Sumaré Study Centre, Rio de Janeiro, 28 July 2013.

11　John (Jan) Berchmans (1599–1621) was a Jesuit canonized by Pope Leo XIII in 1888. On 24 September 1618 he took his vows as a Jesuit, and in 1619 he moved to Rome to finish his studies in philosophy at the Collegio Romano, where, having fallen ill, he died only two years later, on 13 August 1621. Faithful to his favourite mottoes – *Age quod agis* ('If you do something, do it well') and *Maximi facere minima* ('Set great store on little things') – he managed to do ordinary things in an extraordinary way, and to become the saint of everyday life.

12　Cf. Jorge Mario Bergoglio, *È l'amore che apre cli occhi* (Milan, Rizzoli, 2013).

13　*Guarda a la Iglesia de quien fue figura/la inmaculada y maternal María;/ guárdala intacta, firme y con ternura/ de eucaristía.*

14　In the past Pope Francis has paid great attention to educational subjects at various interventions he carried out as cardinal archbishop of Buenos Aires. Cf. Pope Francis, *Nei tuoi ochi è la mia parola. Omelie e discorsi di Buenos Aires 1999–2013* (Milan, Rizzoli, 2016).

Chapter 2 Go Out to the Peripheries of Existence

1 Cf. *My Door is Always Open.*

Chapter 3 A Shepherd's Footsteps

1 Antonio Quarracino (1923–1998) was an Italian Catholic cardinal and archbishop who worked in Argentina from 1945. On 27 June 1992 he consecrated Jorge Mario Bergoglio as a bishop.
2 José Maria di Paola, better known as Father Pepe, was appointed parish priest in Villa 21, a suburb of Buenos Aires, by the then archbishop, Jorge Mario Bergoglio.
3 The *Sancrosanctum Concilium* is the constitution of the Second Vatican Council on the sacred liturgy, promulgated by Paul VI on 4 December 1963.

Chapter 4 Not Everything in Life is Black and White

1 The *Suscipe* is a prayer that St Ignatius inserted in his *Spiritual Exercises* in the so-called *Contemplatio ad amorem* (no. 234): 'Take, Lord, and receive all my liberty, my memory, my understanding, and my entire will, all I have and call my own. You have given all to me. To you, Lord, I return it. Everything is yours; do with it what you will. Give me only your love and your grace, that is enough for me.' We should also remember that Benedict XVI had also recommended the Ignatian *Suscipe*, replying to the seminarians during a visit to the Roman Major Seminary on 17 February 2007.

2   Here the Pontiff is referring to a text by Hugo Rahner produced after a session of studies into Ignatian spirituality. Francis is referring to the reflections that Fr Rahner wrote in the eighth chapter of the volume. Note that the third chapter of the same study was quoted by the Blessed Paul VI on 3 December 1974, addressing the 32nd General Congregation of the Society of Jesus.

Chapter 5 Distance Makes Us Ill

1   The Swede Maria Elisabeth Hesselblad (1870–1957) founded the congregation of the sisters of the Order of the Most Holy Saviour of St Bridget, and was canonized on 5 June 2016.
2   The principle, enshrined after the peace of Augsburg (1555), established the obligation for subjects to follow the confession (Catholic or Reformed) of the governors of the state.
3   The reference is to the Joint Declaration on the Doctrine of Justification, drawn up by Catholic and Lutheran theologians and published in Augsburg on 31 October 1999.
4   'Thirst for Peace: Religions and Cultures in Dialogue', an international meeting held in Assisi between 18 and 20 September 2016, 30 years after the Day of Prayer for Peace organized by John Paul II (27 October 1986).
5   30 July 2016 (cf. previous interview).

Chapter 6 Have Courage and Prophetic Daring

1   *Parresia* is a Greek word that occurs frequently in the Greek text of the New Testament. It indicates the courage and sincerity of the testimony. It is a word widely used in

the Christian tradition, especially in its early days, sometimes in opposition to 'hypocrisy'.

2   In the Ignatian tradition, the *magis* ('the more, the greatest') comes from the famous maxim *ad maiorem Dei gloriam* ('to the greater glory of God') and synthesizes a strong spiritual impulse. The work of the Jesuit is characterized by this *magis*, a living tension that reminds us that it is always possible to take a step forward from where we are, because our walking is in line with an ever more explicit manifestation of the glory of God. With the discernment of spirits we learn to recognize the good that dwells in each situation and to choose the path that leads to the greater good.

3   The Jesuits Matteo Ricci (1552–1610) and Roberto de Nobili (1577–1656) were true pioneers. Missionaries in China and India, respectively, they sought to adapt the proclamation of the Gospel to local culture and worship. But this caused some concern and, in the Church, voices were raised against the spirit of this behaviour, as if it were a contamination of the Christian message.

4   The Pope is referring to the theoretical debates of the early 1600s, in which Jesuits such as Rodrigo de Arriaga were involved.

5   *Cuco* might be translated as 'bogeyman'.

6   Bernard Häring (1922–1998), a Redemptorist, was a German moral theologian and one of the founders of the Accademia Alfonsiana. His work had a significant influence on the preparation and development of Second Vatican Council.

Chapter 7 Take the Gospel Without Tranquillizers

1   A *cilice* is a penitential garment such as a hair shirt.

CHAPTER 9 AT THE CROSSROADS OF HISTORY

1   Pope Paul VI said: 'Wherever in the Church, even in the most difficult and extreme fields, at the crossroads of ideologies, in the social trenches, there has been and there is confrontation between the burning exigencies of man and the perennial message of the Gospel, here also there have been, and there are, Jesuits.' (Paul VI, *Address to the 32nd General Congregation of the Jesuits*, 3 December 1974; ORE, 12 December, n. 2, p. 4.)

2   Pope Francis, *Adesso fate le vostre domande. Conversazioni sulla Chiesa e sul mondo di domani* (Milan, Rizzoli, 2017), p. 8.

CHAPTER 10 WHERE HAVE OUR PEOPLE BEEN CREATIVE?

1   Fr Lorenzo Ricci (1703–1775) carried out the role of Superior General of the Society of Jesus at a delicate moment in the history of the Society owing to tensions with European governments. In his time the Order was expelled first from countries such as Portugal, France and Spain. It was only with Clement XIV that the Society was suppressed, and while Jesuits were integrated into diocesan and religious clergy, Fr Ricci was imprisoned in Castel Sant'Angelo. He lived there alone and was the victim of all sorts of humiliations, maintaining until his death two years later that the Society had given no cause for its suppression.

2   Fr Jan Philippe Roothaan (1783/85–1853) was a Dutch Jesuit and Superior General of the Order (the second after its restoration) from 9 July 1829 until his death. His work as Superior General was very fruitful for the newly restored Order. His chief attention was given to maintaining and

strengthening the spirit of the Society. Nine of his 11 general letters were dedicated to this theme. He enlarged the work in the missions. The Order doubled the number of its members, reaching 5,000 professions. But the Society had to suffer expulsion from many countries, especially in 1848, the year of revolutions.

3   Fr Alonso de Barzana (1530–1597) was assigned the mission of Juli on the banks of Lake Titicaca, in what is today south-eastern Peru. He remained in the central zone of what is now Bolivia for 11 years until he was sent to Tucumán. He carried out missionary work among the Indians of the Valley of Calchaquies and then in Gran Chaco until 1593. He continued his work among the many tribes of that region and those of Paraguay until 1589. He knew many indigenous languages and wrote grammars, dictionaries and catechisms for most of them.

4   Senderoso Luminoso (the Shining Path), or the Communist Party of Peru of the Shining Path of Mariátegui, is a Peruvian guerrilla organization inspired by Maoism, set up between 1969 and 1970 by Abimael Guzmán following a split from the Partido Comunista del Peru – Bandera Roja. Sendero Luminoso seeks to subvert the Peruvian political system and set up socialism through armed confict.

ACKNOWLEDGEMENTS

The publishers are grateful to Libreria Editrice Vaticana for permission to include the Preface by Pope Francis.

They are also grateful to *La Civiltà Cattolica* for permission to publish the last three chapters in the book and to Michael Kelly SJ of UCANews for permission to publish the translations of these chapters. www.ucanews.com.

NOTE ON THE TYPE

The text of this book is set in Linotype Sabon, a type-face named after the type founder, Jacques Sabon. It was designed by Jan Tschichold and jointly developed by Linotype, Monotype and Stempel in response to a need for a typeface to be available in identical form for mechanical hot metal composition and hand compos-ition using foundry type.

Tschichold based his design for Sabon roman on a font engraved by Garamond, and Sabon italic on a font by Granjon. It was first used in 1966 and has proved an enduring modern classic.